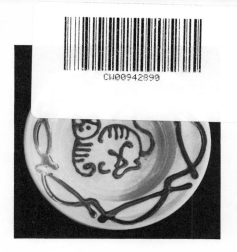

Mary Wondrausch
on **Slipware**

CW00942890

MARY WONDRAUSCH ON SLIPWARE

a potters approach

A & C Black · London

First published 1986
A & C Black (Publishers) Ltd
35 Bedford Row, London WC1R 4JH

© 1986 Mary Wondrausch

Designed and produced by
Alphabet & Image Ltd, Sherborne, Dorset

All rights reserved.
No part of this publication may be reproduced,
stored in a retrieval system, or transmitted, in any
form or by any means, electronic, mechanical,
photocopying, recording or otherwise, without the
prior permission in writing of A & C Black
(Publishers) Ltd.

British Library Cataloguing in Publication Data
Wondrausch, Mary
    Mary Wondrausch on slipware
    1. Slipware
    I. Title
    738.1   NK4285
    ISBN 0-7136-2813-8

ISBN 0-7136-2813-8

Printed in Great Britain by
BAS Printers Limited, Over Wallop, Hampshire
Bound in Great Britain

*The illustration on the front cover shows
a St George and Dragon bowl by the author*

For Diana and Barney Miller

Contents

Plate by the author, dark honey glaze, 15″ diameter, 1984. *Coll. Rev. Norman Smith.*

Acknowledgments

I would like to express my thanks to the
following. To Ron Cooper, for his continued
encouragement, friendship and help; Dr Maria
Kresz for introducing me to Hungary and its
slipwares; Janet Rutter, the archaeologist from
Chester who over the years has shared her
knowledge with me; Jane Turner for tirelessly
typing and organizing me; my daughter Claudia
for her time and stringent comments; Revd
Norman Smith for the loan of so much of his
incomparable collection of books on ceramics;
John Daniels for many of the excellent
photographs; Theresia Götting, the Wiesbaden
potter; Hugh Tait of the British Museum; John
Mallet of the Victoria & Albert Museum;
Richard Smith at Manchester; Pat Halfpenny
from Stoke; and Sotheby's Ceramic Department.
It is impossible to name all the museums and
individuals, as there are so many who have
given me information and allowed me to handle
such valuable pots.

Pre-Raphaelite umbrella stand. 25″ high. Sgraffito,
with background cut away under a dark honey glaze.

What is slipware?

What is meant by 'slipware'? It sounds like skating or sliding, not like pottery, and many people seem to be unclear about the meaning of this term.

Firstly, it is lead-glazed earthenware – firing temperature between 890°C and 1100°C. Secondly, the pots are decorated with coloured 'slip' before they are fired in the kiln. Slip is clay mixed with water. If it is used for covering the body of the pot, then I call it pouring slip, or engobe. It has a thin, batter-like consistency and is usually of a contrasting colour to the body clay; for example, white on a red clay.

Slip trailing is the method of decorating the pot with slip from either a cow-horn, a small clay vessel and quill, rubber bulb and pipette, or the 'Mary Wondrausch inner tube and pipette'. For this last technique, thicker slip is used and lightly extruded.

All work that is earthenware and decorated *in any way* with slips before firing is called slipware. This includes sgraffito, which is the technique of scratching through a leather-hard covering slip to reveal the contrasting clay body underneath, or in some cases to reveal another slip applied below, as in Beauvais ware.

There is an additional group of wares that come roughly under the sgraffito heading as the possibilities of the method are explored. For example: brushing different coloured slips on to the leather-hard background; cutting out the background to reveal large areas of the body colour; painting with oxides such as copper and cobalt to enhance the scratched drawing. A combination of all these techniques can be used together on the same pot. Other decorative techniques normally associated with slipware are marbling and feathering, described later in the text.

Slip-decorated earthenware is not to be confused with majolica (or Faience or Delft ware), where the painting is done on top of a tin glaze after the first firing. The common feature of majolica and slipware is that they are both earthenware.

From earliest times, painted slips were used as decoration. The most familiar of these pots came from China, Ancient Greece, Byzantium, Egypt, Italy and also from Britain during the period of Roman domination when the Castor wares from Northamptonshire were made and decorated, as they were in Germany at this time (see page 44).

Lead-glazed, slip-coated wares were imported to Britain from Beauvais and Saintes in France in the fourteenth century and are found in quantity in many excavated sites. Literally hundreds of chafing dishes (coal pots) from Saintes, known as Saintonge wares, have been excavated all over Britain, undecorated except for splashes of glaze. La Chapelle des Pots near Saintes was known for its strange barrel-type wine containers, heavily embossed and lead-glazed. Slipware was made here until the beginning of the twentieth century. Now in the 1980s there is a large factory on the same site, producing jigger and jolleyed and moulded imitation Renaissance and eighteenth-century Faience!

Introduction

Slipware is the oldest and most vibrant of the English folk traditions in pottery. To many people the term slipware means Thomas Toft, who, although one of the most celebrated, was not the only potter working in this medium whose pots are still extant. Simpson, Talor, Wright, Johnson, Malkin and Meir are names inscribed and dated on seventeenth- and eighteenth-century pots. Holding their dishes in one's hands, gazing at the flowing lines, one is filled with respect and amazement, marvelling increasingly at the beautiful effects that were produced in country potteries of the period despite the most daunting circumstances: in cold, ill-protected structures with fire hazards, and where raw materials and finished wares were subject to such appalling transport conditions. Burslem, Harlow, Wrotham, Potovens were towns, Devon, Somerset and Wales were major areas where these wares were made in the seventeenth century.

By the end of the eighteenth century both highly decorated tin-glazed and slipwares ceased to be made in central areas of England, because communications had improved and industrial methods of production were explored, especially in Staffordshire. However, in North Devon the elaborate sgraffito harvest and sheep-shearing jugs and other wares continued to be made well into the early twentieth century. Country potteries in Halifax and Burton in Lonsdale in Yorkshire, Penrith in Cumbria, Buckley and Ewenny in Wales, Burslem in Staffordshire and Rye in Sussex made functional pots decorated with a small amount of trailing, often white on a red body. The period of decorating in the Toft manner probably lasted for only eighty years.

I believe the principal reason for the cessation of elaborate slip-decorated work in England was twofold; firstly, changes in fashion. There was a swing to the classical mode (for example, Wedgwood's Etruria ware) far removed from the ebullient style that Charles II brought with him from France in the 1660s. Secondly, slip-trailing is a very difficult medium and needs not only great skill but also the right workshop conditions, which did not somehow suit the incoming technology. Slips had to be kept in good condition, the cow-horn or 'bucket' clean, the goose quills clear of dried clay: all time-consuming, individual tasks. Added to this, only the 'master' would have the ability to perform the skilled task of decorating the major pieces, although it is quite possible that an assistant would help with the minute white slip-trailed dots, or 'pearling'. It is interesting to see the way these blend so easily into the 'drawing' outlines. Obviously the white pouring slip would have been very wet. The 'jewelling' would have been done extremely quickly, for the dots not to be raised; when confronted with a Thomas Toft dish, all this becomes clear.

In my own experience, if there is a very large dish to be decorated with a lot of jewelling, two or three decorators work together so that the decoration does not, in its final stage, stand out dry from the rest of the work after it is glazed.

Toft wares have a semi-matt surface as a result of being once-fired in the kiln, and because of the reducing atmosphere, where the flames feed on the body, the slip and the glaze. Many of the

Thomas Toft 'The Pelican in her Piety'. 19½″ diameter.

large dishes were fired on edge, but the distortion, on the whole, was fairly minimal. I have followed this example with several 22 inch chargers which would not otherwise fit in my kiln, after wiping the glaze from the small segment of rim that actually touches the kiln shelf.

Now, however, in the late twentieth century when the social need has disappeared, the functional purpose of such earthenware pots is debatable. How can the urge to make and decorate these things be justified? Why should these shining and humorous wares of the past have a special relevance to the potter in the late twentieth century? Partly, I believe, as a reaction against the precision of the machine age, and also partly in response to the rumbustuous enjoyment evident in the naïve quality of the work. It is interesting that in eastern Europe excellent examples of this type of folk art are not only preserved, but are still being made. In Hungary in the nineteenth century, houses, carts and costumes, as well as pots were elaborately embellished. In preparation for the marriage ceremony a bride's dowry, quite unrelated to the economic status of the family, might include the whole output of a kiln – 1000 pieces – as part of the bride's portion.

In this book you will find an outline of the history which helps to place slip-decorated wares in their context, as well as details of the techniques employed. If you are making pots, your work will be enriched by rural traditions, and as you visit museums in this country and abroad, your ideas about the humble potter whose pots so many people describe as crude and ill-made will change.

Earthenware is the most difficult of all ceramic disciplines. It can be compared to working in water-colour as opposed to oil. Everything that you do is final, irrevocable. Fixed in the kiln are all the accidents of glaze application that can be so exciting in stoneware, but in low-fired red clay are a disaster. It is a challenge to both the student and the mature craftsman.

Large dish by the author, to celebrate the Royal Wedding in 1981, dark honey glaze. 19″ diameter.

Part 1 The Practice

1 A small beginning

When I taught in a boys' Preparatory School in the 1960s, I became increasingly dissatisfied with the ambiguous nature of my role, questioning 'art' itself as a subject. Perhaps if I worked in pottery this would prove to be a practical science with simple rules that it would be possible to teach to small boys. I attended Farnham College of Art as a part-time student, and worked slowly through the early ash-glaze-and-Leach syndrome until I came to see that all the effects were created in the kiln. Going against accepted English taste, I found the pots that I saw on long continental holidays more sympathetic.

I discovered Ronald Cooper's book *Slipware Dishes 1650–1850* and visited the Glaisher Collection at the Fitzwilliam Museum in Cambridge. I fell in love with the English work of the seventeenth century. I had painted in

water-colours and the challenge of slip-decorated earthenware was, in a sense, similar. Each mark that you make is irremediable, and there are no kiln accidents to soften or enhance the decoration and glaze.

After three or four years' practice, chance played a major part in my decision to start my own small pottery business. I met someone who wanted to rent the garage behind their shop to

Sketch designs for platters

a craftsman. The rent of £12 per week seemed reasonable and I decided to raise what capital I could, buy a kiln and a wheel, and with the help of COSIRA, set up my workshop and try to make my living as a potter.

There were such disasters: chosen clay bodies became unobtainable, frits were unreliable, my work was often bad. I did not sit and weep, but photographed the better pots and sent pictures to *The Times*, and enquiries began to come in. An order for a thousand ashtrays – all lettered and individually designed – was a great breakthrough. An ex-Farnham student colleague, Dilla Davis, joined me and we worked

Lidded posset 'The best is not too good for you', black and green slip with pearling on white engobe. Seventeenth-century Staffordshire ware.

the work of Thomas Toft made me become a commemorative potter in the first place; making plates with words and pictures recording the outstanding events in people's lives. Initially my designs were derived from folk art sources: the embroidery on Hungarian herdsmen's frieze cloaks, nineteenth-century sailors' embroidered wool pictures, the scratched patterns and stories on sailors' scrimshaws or horn snuff boxes, canal long-boat 'rose and castle' decoration, Scherenschnitte (traditional paper cutting) as practised by the Pennsylvanian Germans, the birds and the flowers and the dancing people covering the Slovak milk jugs. All these sources were the work of untrained people, filling in their time at sea or as they watched the sheep on the mountains.

Another source of inspiration were the strangely still figures with their curling wigs and curling pipes and gartered stockings on the English seventeenth-century Staffordshire slip-trailed plates.

As well as inspiration from costumes, etc., I was influenced by other themes that recur in

from 8 am to 8 pm, staggering to the local pub for a large whisky with Guinness chasers at the end of each day. We were unpacking and re-packing the kiln at 350°C. Fortunately I was lent an extra wheel and then I bought another kiln from a friend.

After one year's extraordinary progress I borrowed enough money from the bank to lease new premises, with a flat above. Renting this apartment paid the rates, and the orders for marriage and birth plates continued to arrive as we wrote for publicity in every kind of journal. I remember a Nationwide TV team turned up the day after we moved.

In 1977, the Jubilee Year, we sold commemorative wares to Liberty's and Harrods in London, and many other shops. At the same time, I was trying to find direct markets, acting completely against the pottery mainstream. This was no Zen situation, dreaming in a country shed, I knew it was necessary to be accessible in the High Street. I had my family to support and no other income.

I can remember how it was that my love for

Moulded dish with tulip and trellis
design. 17″ diameter. Eighteenth-
century Staffordshire ware.

THE
TULIP

ceramics from Turkey to Burslem, including, for
instance, the tulip. I am certain this was not
used as a drawing from nature but for the
flexibility of its design possibilities. Few, if any,
potters would actually have seen one of them in
bloom. The drawings alongside show some of
those designs used on English slipware pots in
the seventeenth century. The tulip as a form was
first used when the bulb was imported into
Britain in the seventeenth century and
subsequently became a mania. Paintings,
embroideries, silks for clothes, silver objects, as
well as huge tin-glaze tulipières (many-sided
and spouted vases) were all made at this period
to hold or depict the flowers. I have read that
the tulip was the Arab symbol of love. Perhaps
it is : in any event, its simplified form has been
used by potters all over Europe and in the Near
East as a motif either painted, scratched or
trailed on the surface of every kind of pot, and
it is often incorporated into my own work.

Somehow all these people, birds and flowers
had rigorously to conform to design criteria. For
example the hands of the bridegroom have to be

raised to fill the gap on the right of the dish, the bride must loop her arm to hold the bouquet of flowers on the left, not for any symbolic reason but simply to fill an awkward space.

When thinking of inspiration, I remember a fellow potter who postulated that his ideas came from three sources: from nature, from nowhere and from technique.

Taking each of these three sources in turn, I find that I get absolutely no direct inspiration from nature, despite the fact that I live in a beautiful rural situation and am surrounded by nesting birds and blossom. When I have to draw oak trees, for instance, or apple trees, they become the most simplified form of a tree, similar to those found in Renaissance tapestries or illuminated manuscripts. Nevertheless, as I work, I think of the oak or apple as I remember it and hope that the resultant design has an undeniable 'appleness' about it.

When it comes to ideas from nowhere, I do not think I am the kind of potter who works in the abstract. The shapes that I make are all functional shapes: a two-pint jug, a salt kit, or an egg stand. It is the function that defines the

Right a salt kit, with sgraffito design, clear glaze with manganese. 7″ high, 1983. *Below* egg stands for six eggs and individual eggs, sgraffito and slip trail, 1985.

form, and the form the decoration. The ideas for my pots are definitely from *somewhere*. They derive principally from eighteenth- and nineteenth-century pots where their function was a vital part of people's daily lives: the work in the dairy, the slaughter of a pig, the washing of clothes and dishes, the storage of water, wine or oil. Because of this, the pots have a 'holiness' that I admire, a rightness about them, so that even if they are put to other uses they still retain some of their initial goodness.

Nothing I make comes 'off the top of my head' and I never endeavour to make something that has never been done before. I do not believe this is possible. (Perhaps my life and work as a painter when I was younger, with all its striving for unique expression, has satiated these abstract needs and I no longer have to make Fine Art objects.) Instead, I am in thrall to the clay, humble before its amazing capacities. How can ideas come from *nowhere*?

13

Left commemorative wedding plate by the author, based on a Restoration couple – see page 11.

Above design for a cheese platter motif, and, *below,* cheese platter with still-life design by the author, sgraffito, polychrome, clear glaze, 9″ diameter, 1985.

As for technique as a source for design, this has relevance for the earthenware potter, particularly as he extends and elaborates the various trailing, scratching and painting methods of decoration. But the mark of the tool is not the catalyst, and as far as I am concerned it is the story that I am commissioned to produce, and the new ways of interpreting the idea, which excite me.

So, for a slipware potter, where decoration is a vital part of the discipline, much of the inspiration comes from the client who wants not only a particular object, such as a jug or a plate, but a specific record of a memorable occasion.

For a potter the client imposes constraints which can often prove a source of strength. There are similarities between these and the limitations proposed by the architect's client. I have drawn Pekinese and Yorkshire terriers, saddleback pigs, and boathouses, and from these unlikely subjects I have found ways to make new designs – with humour but, I hope, integrity.

Alongside the commissioned work in my studio there are the regular 'lines', such as the flat platters made to display cheese with the names of cheeses round the rims; writing them I remember their taste and smell and where I bought and ate them.

I seldom do a detailed preliminary sketch and

Hanging bowls, 5½″ diameter, by the author, white slip trail on black engobe, dark honey glaze.

mark out or 'trace' designs on the pot. I find vitality is lost through excessive preparation. Instead, I always work with a reference in front of me, either a previous pot or a relevant photograph. However, certain pottery forms exact a certain discipline in technique. Often, for instance, the limitations of the tool combined with the shape of the pot prevent one from producing a delicate decoration inside a small deep bowl.

Designs for the central motif for a cheese platter *(above)* **and commemorative plate** *(right)* **by the author.**

2 Techniques

Clays

For the earthenware potter the choice of a clay body is vital, because a fit is required not only with the final clear glaze (crazing, often acceptable in stoneware, disfigures earthenware) but also with the pouring slip (engobe) and other trailing slips. After my two initial attempts at finding the perfect material failed, and on the advice of Ray Finch, I ordered a trial sample of Fremington clay from North Devon. This proved to be a beautiful plastic clay for throwing, and Brannams, the suppliers, could provide a well-fitting white clay (Bideford Pipe Clay) for the slip.

These are the basic materials that I use, but readers far from these sources will have to follow the same course as I did in finding good materials. Try locally available clays, and ask the advice of nearby potters.

Fremington firing 980°C–1060°C, vitrifying at 1100°C.

Fremington is a glacial sedimentary clay; a large mass of clay of Pleistocene Age found sitting on top of rocks of Carboniferous Age in North Devon. This clay is marvellous for throwing hollow wares as it retains its shape so well.

There is no sand or grog present in Fremington clay, so the shrinkage rate is high – about one eighth. This makes it unsuitable for throwing larger plates: the rims dry more quickly than the base, so there is often cracking. This problem would probably not be so acute in a large pottery with a damp room, but in a small workshop, where the kilns are firing, keeping earthenware sufficiently damp is a major problem. Very slow drying is the only answer for plates that are about 14 inches in diameter, and this is difficult where there is very little space available.

The suppliers, C. H. Brannams of Litchdon Pottery, Barnstaple, Devon, will provide a sanded body at extra cost, but this is more suitable for garden wares. It is excellent for these, as the clay does not encourage the growth of algae on the flowerpot.

Potclays 1135 firing 1150°C, vitrifying at 1130°C.

This is a red, slightly sanded body. It is recommended for the larger flat wares, where the shrinkage is not so acute, and allows more flexibility in the firing temperature. As far as slip is concerned, Bideford Pipe Clay for pouring (Brannams) and TWVD (Watts, Blake & Bearne of Newton Abbot, Devon) both fit this body equally well. I do not recommend it for throwing hollow areas as it is inclined to be 'short'. It is useful, with 10 per cent extra grog, for garden pots.

Reclaiming Clay

It is a good thing to keep all your turnings and scrapings of clay in an open bucket and not to slake down until they are quite dry. We keep a small lidded dustbin under the sink where we pour the water from the throwing slurry, and to this the dry clay is added.

When a thick slurry is formed, scoop it up in your hands into bisqued bowls and leave to dry in the open air until it is almost of leather consistency. Then put it into fertiliser sacks, date the label with a waterproof marker and keep for six months. Then mix the hard and the soft clay alternately and put through a pug-mill. This can produce an excellent body.

When our mix has a predominance of Fremington, we use it for hollow wares. If the clay is redder (predominance of Potclays) it is better used for flat wares.

Keeping the clay clean

It must always be borne in mind that you will be spending a long time decorating a commissioned plate, so the condition of your clay body is all important. If you are doing sgraffito decoration, splinters of wood off the bats, or sand and grit from the floor and garden, deflect your tool and make a hesitant line which detracts from the immediacy of the drawing.

Techniques

Equally, when you are turning a plate or bowl, any stone in the body leaves a deep groove as your turning tool drags it around.

It is preferable not to use grog in a pottery where the mass of work is decorated, but if you do have to use it for garden ware or tiles it is advisable to clean up carefully, as grog is ubiquitous — weeks later nasty grooves will appear on the base of turned bowls and the turnings will crop up again in the reclaimed body six months later. The wheel should be cleaned after use, and all grogged clay waste kept labelled and in a plastic sack of distinctive colour. If grog is to be used, "60's" is recommended, as it is very fine.

Throwing tools.

doubly important to have sufficient space under the pot for the glaze to clear the raised lines — on no account must a spot of glaze touch the kiln shelf. To ensure enough clay, allow 1·4 kg for a 9 inch plate, and 3 kg for a 12 inch plate. Use the minimum amount of water for throwing, only wetting your hands and *not* splashing cupfuls of slurry on to the clay.

Throwing plates for slip decorating

Use a smooth body and throw with far more clay than you imagine necessary, as you will need this extra amount of clay both to support the rim and to allow for a deep foot. The plate will be decorated on the bat before turning, and after turning you will be piercing the foot rim for hanging; and if the pot is sufficiently moist, not only signing but trailing a small picture on the base. This gives a very special surprise to your customer, and it is fun for you to do a quick free sketch with the white trailer. For this, it is

Shaping a plate with the hand and a wooden rib.

Techniques

A good broad rim to the plate will accommodate two bands of slip and lettering if required. The edge of the plate itself needs to be bold, both for the look and to prevent curling.

The weight of your clay ball, the size of your throwing bat and the dimensions of your rib (see below) and measuring stick will all define the finished article, as will the depth needed in the foot rim to support the pierced hole and keep the glaze clear from the kiln shelf.

The pictures show how the fingers are used to improve the shape of the rim.

Above a hefty amount of clay is left under the rim and base to support the weight of engobe and to allow a deep foot rim after turning.

Above a wooden rib improves the profile of the plate and makes the 'change of direction' crisp.

Preparation of slips

The word 'slip' is commonly used for the liquid poured into vessels to make the background colour. To avoid confusion, in this book the more appropriate word 'engobe' is used for this throughout the text.

Pouring Slip or Engobe

For white background engobe, I use Bideford Pipe Clay which comes to my pottery exactly as quarried (damp and full of earth, roots and grit) from C. H. Brannams in Barnstaple, Devon. It is an interesting clay as its name denotes; it was the clay used for making moulded pipes, probably from as early as the seventeenth century. To me it brings two great benefits; firstly it fits perfectly both the Potclays 1135 and the Fremington throwing clay. There is never any sign of peeling. The second pleasure is that it is not dead white. After sieving, the colour is a kind of greyish ivory, and the residual impurities in the clay make for a certain liveliness in the finished pot. Because the firing is done in an oxidizing atmosphere in an electric kiln, there are none of the flashes of colour or changes of texture that you get in wood or coal firing, or indeed with once-fired wares.

There is always Bideford clay drying in large biscuited dishes on top of the kiln. We use a throwing wire to cut off thin slices from this lump to put in the pans. It needs to be completely dry before pounding in a large mortar. I have tried placing it between newspaper on the floor and leaping on it to break it up (not entirely successful), or rolling it between linen cloths, but the mortar is best. Pound just a little clay at a time, and when it is like large cake crumbs pour it into a bucket of hot water. It is best then to leave it for a week, stirring it by hand once a day.

When you have the time, someone to talk to, or a good programme on the radio, start brushing it through a 100-mesh sieve.* Try and get a friend to do it again the next day through the 120-mesh sieve. (This is a boring job.) You have to keep your eye on the resulting dustbin of engobe as it is surprising how quickly it gets used up. So, whenever there is nothing else to do, start slicing or pounding or stirring the next lot of engobe to make sure that there is always some in reserve.

It is difficult to describe in words the consistency of any material. Often culinary terms are helpful – a slightly thicker than usual pancake batter is a good comparison. Dr Plot in his *History of Staffordshire 1686* described it thus:

> '. . . which none of three other clays they call slips will any of them doe, being of looser and more friable natures. These [clays] mixed with water they make into a consistence thinner than a syrup so that being put in a bucket it will run through a quill. This they call slip and is the substance which they paint their wares.'

Trailing slip

For use in the slip-trailer, or in my case the Mary Wondrausch cycle inner-tube, I use about seven different colours, all of which are based on natural clays, sometimes with the addition of oxides.

Red slip It is a good idea to save the turnings of ungrogged wares. Keep them in a dry sack, then slake them in a bucket of hot water. The resultant slurry needs sieving through both 100- and 120-mesh sieves because of the coarseness of the clay.

White slip I recommend and use TWVD from Watts, Blake & Bearne of Newton Abbot, Devon. They produce ball clays which are very pure with almost a bluish quality. The origin of the name 'ball-clay' is interesting, and dates back to the time when the clay was transported

---

* 100-mesh is a gauge of fineness in the phosphor-bronze mesh used in pottery sieves or lawns. It is non-metric and means 100 strands to the inch.

by packhorse and then by sea for export. It was made up into balls, and eight of these fitted into a horse's panier.

The secret of making a good slip is to sprinkle the ball clay on the surface of the water and gradually let it be absorbed into the liquid. Only a 120-mesh sieve is needed for this and it is easier to have a jug of water at hand to add as you are brushing it through the sieve. Always make these slips a day or two before you need them as water can easily be taken off the surface if it is too thin. Submerge a clean jug carefully into the centre of the bucket fractionally below the surface, and you will find that the water fills the jug without disturbing the suspended material below.

Black slip My recipe for this is 9 kg red clay body, 1 kg manganese, 500g red iron oxide, and 500g flint, which needs to be brushed through both 100- and 120-mesh sieves.

I like this slip as it is nearer in tone to those used in seventeenth- and eighteenth-century pots, both here and on the Continent. Some people use cobalt in their black slip which does make an intense black colour with a greenish tinge, but I prefer the warm brownish tone achieved by my mixture.

Dark brown slip is a mixture of all the trailing slips squeezed out when you are testing the flow of your trailers. I keep an old plastic tray by the wheel for this purpose when I am decorating.

Blue slip 4 per cent of cobalt carbonate is added to the dry TWVD ball-clay powder. For example, 40g cobalt carbonate to 10 kg TWVD. Add this as usual to half a bucket of warm water, stir and then brush through a 120-mesh sieve. As this slip only appears as a dull grey, and can give a misleading impression before it is fired, I add a small amount of liquid blue dye (Kenalake Blue 2GL from Durham Chemicals) to colour it. This is most helpful when you are decorating.

This slip is a bright blue under clear glaze, but with dark honey glaze it is a very rich bottle-green. There is a lot of room for experiment here – anything from 0.5 to 6 per cent cobalt carbonate will give shades from pale olive to indigo. However, any form of cobalt is expensive.

Further colours can be achieved by mixing the slips. For *orange* slip mix approximately 3 parts red to 2 parts white; for *cream* slip use 1 part red to 7 parts white; and for *ochre* slip use 7 parts white to 1 part black.

Trailing slips should be kept in close-covered containers. We never make up too much at one time, and old-fashioned enamel cake and flour bins are very acceptable. The plastic, very tight-fitting lidded containers are unsuitable for daily use as their lids are so hard to get off, but they are excellent for transporting or keeping rarely used experimental slips. Always label everything with masking tape and waterproof pen on both lid and bucket.

It saves a lot of work if you keep a little plastic or enamel cup in the bucket for filling your trailers. Wipe down the inside walls of the bucket after using the slip, as this will prevent caked particles falling into the liquid and postpone the need to resieve.

Each slip probably needs topping up and sieving about every 3 or 4 weeks – one of many reasons why there are so many stoneware potters!

Techniques

All these slips with the addition of water can be used for a pouring engobe, but it does get complicated and you use up a tremendous amount of space and containers. Generally speaking, I use only the black and the blue as engobes and they are both mixed to a thinner consistency than usual for this, because they cover the red body better than the white Bideford slip.

Slip is poured on to a large plate and swirled around while it is still attached to the bat. Holding it by the bat, the slip is poured back into the bin and the last drops are shaken off.

The top picture shows a salt kit being removed from the slip after dipping the top part. The lower picture shows the potter preparing to dip the bottom half.

Decoration

Slip-trailing is the most difficult of all methods of decoration. In the seventeenth century and earlier, the potters used a clay vessel which was filled through a narrow neck and had a small opening on one side through which a quill was inserted. Alternatively they used a horn, carefully chosen to be as upright as possible to avoid spillage. With both these tools the slip would have to be poured with a tipping motion.

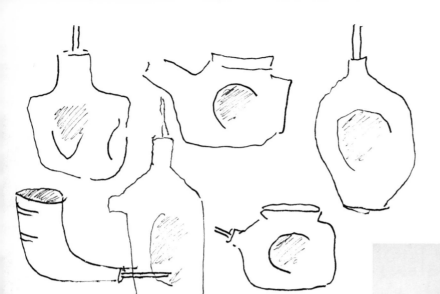

Eighteenth-century continental earthenware, glazed 'buckets' or slip trailers, and, *left,* a horn.

The pearling on a Toft plate is miniscule, and as many of these dishes were at least 20 inches in diameter it must have been an exhausting business tipping the horn to make tiny drops over the whole outline drawing. It would have been possible to have made a slightly thicker slip and to have used a wider goose quill, but there is still no mechanism for extruding the material and the only control was tipping up the container.

'Mary Wondrausch slip trailers'; inner tube, bulldog clip, cork, and ball-point pen.

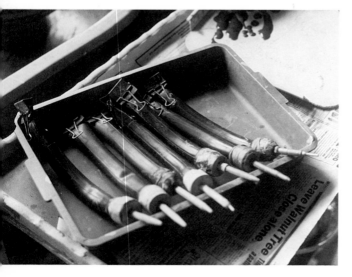

Slip trail designs from the 1950s by John Solly. The fish plate has blue and black trailing on ivory engobe.

When this method of decoration was revived in the 1930s and 1950s, a rubber bulb with a removable glass nozzle was used and later a simple ear syringe, both of which suck in the air and then let it out with a sound like breaking wind, splattering slip all over the dish. Consequently I have invented the infamous MW trailer concocted out of waste materials: inner tubes, paper clips, corks and ball-point pens. Recently I have discovered fine plastic pipettes available from German pottery suppliers or English laboratory suppliers. Although very fine, these do not have the continuous easy flow that my own nozzles have when in use.

A slip trailer is filled to the top with thick black slip. The inner tube is folded over, *right*, while it is still full, to ensure that there is no air inside. The bulldog clip is fastened and, *far right*, the full trailer is ready to be washed clean.

Slip-trailing : the preparation

When all the thick slips are in perfect condition, the trailers should be emptied from the clip end into their respective colours. Then the nozzles are cleaned out from the broad end with a fine crisp feather under the running tap, being careful not to split or dislodge the fine tip.

Overfill each trailer with the slip so that no air can get into the tube. Fold over the rubber end and snap on the clip. Lay this under the tap until it is clean then put on an old towel. Fill all your trailers in succession, depending on the

The nozzle end of the Mary Wondrausch trailer and, *below*, alternative German pipettes.

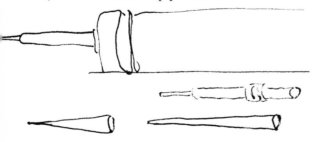

number of colours that you want to use. It may take up to forty minutes.

It is advisable to slip the plates before filling the trailers (see pages 20–21). The plates will still be attached to their bats and it is very simple to swill the engobe gently round the plate, tip it over the edge, then wipe off any surplus under the rim and on the bat with a small sponge. Generally speaking, thirty minutes should elapse before the plates are decorated : after that time the shine has almost disappeared and you are ready to work. None of these rules is finite as so much depends on the workshop atmosphere. If the telephone rings or a customer comes in to give an order, the work will have to wait and will probably not suffer too much.

Decorating a plate As a beginner, never approach decoration without having designed and sketched out your lettering and central motif. Practice will tell you the number of words that fit into the rim, and, if you are hesitant, pour some white slip over one of your round bats and with your black trailer make two outer bands about an inch apart to simulate your

23

plate. Then see how the lettering fits. The trick is always to end up with a date, thus:

Venetia and Anthony were married on 24th of May 1986
Venetia and Anthony were married on 24–5–1986
Venetia and Anthony were married 24–5–86

You will then be sure you can fit in the complete inscription.

The most difficult part is not allowing the nozzle of your trailer to touch the slip on the plate. A very gentle pressure is continuously exerted.

If you take your hands off the trailer suddenly it will draw the air into it, subsequently splattering slip over the pot. That is why each time, after I have lifted the trailer from the plate to start a new motif or fill in with different colours, I extrude a small amount on to my 'trial' tray (these trials are later brushed with a rubber kidney into the mixed slip container), and still keeping my hands in that position and exerting the same pressure, I continue to work on the plate. Never gesticulate with the trailer in your hand or get a friend to pass you something over the wet plate! In between decorative additions, always lift up your trailer and gently wipe the drip which develops off the tip of the nozzle.

Do not alter a drawing on the plate. If you make a mistake wash it off, slip another plate and start again.

The slipware potter plunges into his decoration with a recognizable élan. The tools of his trade do not allow for an intellectual approach, a slow summing-up of the possibilities. As soon as the first shine is off the engobe, he must get on with the job.

This is the best sequence of events. Band your rim first, then trail in your outline, then pearl the banding with little blobs of white slip. Make sure the nozzle does not touch the black slip band. By the time you have done this, your outline design will have firmed up and you can begin to fill in the body colours. Work one colour at a time, placing the colours in a balanced way in blodges over the whole pattern. Repeat this method with each colour, working through the spectrum from dark to light: blue, dark brown, red, orange, ochre and cream.

The best method is to work on a plate that has been thrown on the previous afternoon. If kept in a damp area, it will be just right for decorating the morning after throwing, and by the late afternoon is ready for wiring off and placing on an absorbent bat. This is a nerve-racking process because at this stage the plate is so wet it sags in the middle. With a 12 inch diameter or larger plate, someone will have to help you. Both of you must slide your hands under the body of the plate, being careful not to touch the rim, then flop it gently on to the absorbent bat.

This method dries the plate underneath at a similar rate to the rim. Remember there should be about 1 inch thickness of clay on the base to

A spelling mistake mars a fishy plate.

be turned off later. I seldom turn a plate over
to dry as it is important not to damage the
decorated rim or let it dry too quickly. It is
possible to enclose it gently in a clean plastic bag
while its base rests on the drying bat.
Subsequently it will be possible to turn the pot
the next day and put it to dry.

Day 1 – 4 pm		Throw 9 inch or 12 inch plates on bats. Put in cool area.
Day 2 – 10 am		Slip plates still on throwing bats. Fill trailers.
	10.30 am	Decorate.

The top picture shows the rim design being trailed.
Above the outline of the motif. *Right* filling in the
cockerel with coloured slips.

Techniques

5 pm	Wire off, and move plates on to absorbent bats, with help if necessary. Keep in cool area.
Day 3 – 12 noon	Turn off surplus clay, on 9 inch plate (about 500g) and pierce foot rim, sign and decorate underneath with white trailer.

The 12 inch plate will take an extra day or two to dry.

Everyone's workshop is unique, so there can be no definite rules except that on the whole it is better to keep the pot in a cool atmosphere rather than near the kiln or out in the sun.

Every commemorative piece has its own special character, just as your client has.

One of the greatest satisfactions a craftsman gets in the direct relationship with his customer is seeing the pleasure something so personal gives.

Tea poys with inlay decoration from Brede in Sussex, late nineteenth century.

Other methods of slip decoration

Inlay as in Sussex ware. This involves cutting out the pattern with a looped tool, to produce a lowered surface, then filling with thick white slip and carefully scraping down the surface. It is a technique with various possibilities.

In Chailey, Sussex, they used metal type, both letters and ornament. This can often be purchased from your local printer as printers have now adopted photographic methods of reproduction. Nevertheless, it is a method of decoration to be used only by the extremely fastidious worker, as unless the type is pressed into the body with mathematical precision the result is unattractive. To keep the image clear, it is necessary to remove every scrap of surplus white clay from the surface. This seems best done with a steel kidney. Using a grogged body often leaves unsightly scratches. On the whole, a free-hand approach is more successful for anyone who wishes to try inlay work.

Sprigging from plaster moulds in contrasting clays. Familiar to many on the Nottingham brown saltglazed wares, but used infrequently on earthenware.

Feathering This is usually done on flat slabs of rolled clay laid on a cloth. The base slip is poured over the whole slab at an angle, letting the surplus fall into a wide-mouthed container.

Above left the holes for stringing a plate have to be bored in the foot rim while the clay is leather-hard. The picture *left* shows the stringing and a slip-trailed design on the underside of a pot.

Techniques

Then place the board on your work surface and immediately start trailing lines of contrasting slip from left to right; then turn your board around at a right angle and draw the stripped feather carefully and evenly across the lines. You can then turn the board again and feather in the opposite direction, if you wish. When the slab is dry enough not to be damaged by contact, yet supple enough to take shape, place it pattern-side down over a very smooth biscuited hump mould, trim the edges with a frog, and the next day you can make a 'pie crust' frill round the edge with a wooden tool, if you wish.

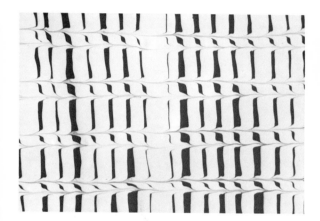

Using a stripped feather, the author demonstrates the technique of feathering across white slip-trailed lines on black engobe, with the result shown *left*.

A press-moulded dish with pie-crust edge, feathered white on black engobe, on buff body under a clear glaze. Early twentieth-century, Staffordshire.

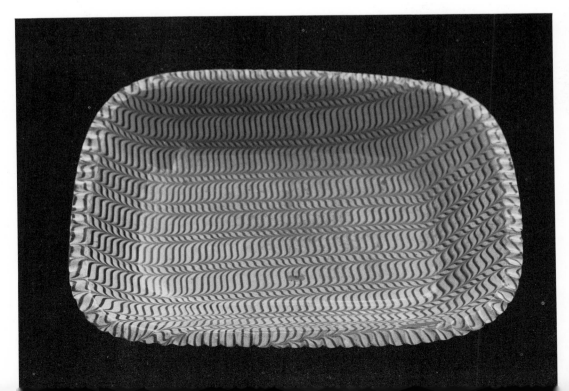

John Pollex teapot, height 5½″. Bright coloured brushed slip on black engobe, under a clear glaze.

Slip combing is done with either a rubber or wooden tool on the revolving wheelhead through the very wet pouring slip/engobe. This is a much more skilled operation than it would at first appear. Michael Cardew has made wonderful use of this economic decoration on his pots.

Marbling is called 'joggling' in the museum world, an adjective that very adequately describes the process. Coat the plate with the white Bideford engobe, and while it is still very wet, trail on a few widely spaced lines of a contrasting slip and gently move the plate around, causing a pattern to emerge, and then pour off the surplus. It is difficult to achieve a good sharp black and white contrast initially as, when you are inexperienced, the slips will often merge into an overall muddy colour. Like all the other skills the slipware potter has to master, this particular technique will take time.

Surface marbling is not to be confused with agate ware, where the different clay bodies themselves are marbled.

Slip painting This technique is complicated, as the brush strokes of clay have to be built up to provide solid colour. One stroke will burn away

in the firing to produce a mere shadow, and each layer of colour has to be left partially to dry before the next is applied. Wonderful abstract effects can be produced by this method, but it is for the patient person as it is very time consuming and will result in endless trial and error before any satisfactory results can be achieved.

Impressing is an ancient technique, illustrated in the seventeenth-century Wrotham ware and some Toft jugs. A notched stick was pressed into the thick, leather-hard trailed slip to produce a raised and patterned effect.

Once you have learnt — and it can take a long time — the trick of feathering, blobbing, combing, etc., it is just a skill like graining or scumbling wood, and not demanding enough for the creative artist. I prefer the words and the illustrative content which can be produced by the more elaborate, less automatic, methods of trailing and scratching.

An eighteenth-century Staffordshire owl jug illustrates the technique of feathering and marbling all over the three-dimensional surface.

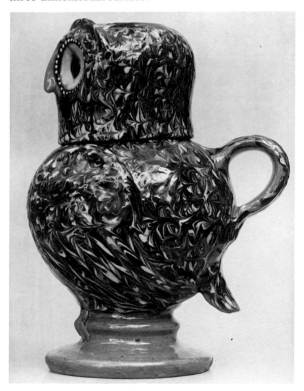

A tyg (drinking vessel) dated 1656, from Wrotham,
showing slip trailed, applied and stamped decoration,
under a honey glaze.

The technique of sgraffito

The word sgraffito means 'scratched', and for
the slipware potter it is, generally speaking,
scratching through white engobe while it is at
the leather-hard stage to reveal the red body
underneath.

Far more discipline is needed to draw on pots
with a pointed tool than to trail on them. Only
the very crispest decoration is satisfactory. An
undiscovered spelling mistake means the pot has
to be thrown away.

The hollow wares to be scratched should be
slipped the previous evening and they will be
dry enough to handle the next day. I used to
hold the pots by the base and dip them neck-
down in the engobe, but this left rather untidy
finger marks on the base and an uneven flow of
slip inside the pot. Latterly I have been using
two different approaches.

1 Place the hand firmly inside the mug or jug
   and gently dip it into the engobe base-down.
   Make sure it is absolutely vertical and the
   engobe comes up to the rim all round the pot.
   Lift it out, still with just the one hand, shake
   it once or twice to get rid of any surplus
   engobe and wipe the base on a piece of damp
   foam resting on a firm board.

Slip decoration trailed, brushed and applied on a
model kitchen. 8 × 4″, by the author. Clear glaze.

Above right holding the mug at an angle when
shaking off the surplus slip prevents a build-up
under the handle. *Right* the slip is cleaned from
the base on a piece of foam rubber.

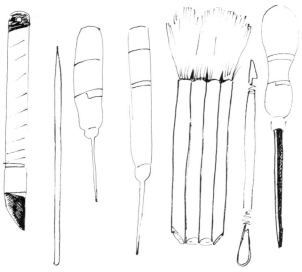

Tools used for sgraffito work.

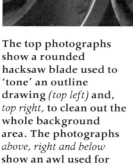

2 Carefully pour white engobe into the mug, tip it out, then just dip the rim again, holding the mug by the base. The next day you will be able to slip the outside in a contrasting colour using the same method as in 1, above.

Flat wares are slipped with the Bideford clay engobe as for trailing, and when dry they may be banded on the wheel. Then the surplus clay is turned off. The rims are brushed with white engobe to remove any marks caused by the turning. I use a small holing tool for banding, holding it so that it faces backwards, as this makes a nice neat little furrow. I keep the end sharpened. If you use a needle-like tool for this process it ploughs up ridges of clay on either side of the line.

The drier you can decorate, the crisper your lines will be and the less residual clay there will be to brush off, but the pot should not be bone dry. For the drawing, I use a tool rather like a small awl which fits right into my hand, bringing me close to the pot when I work on it.

Always decorate the neck or rim of a pot first, as this is the first surface to dry.

There are three basic ways of using the scratch method in earthenware:

1 Making a pointed line through the engobe to reveal the red body beneath.
2 Carefully outlining the design so that the whole background engobe can be cut away, as in the seventeenth to nineteenth-century Bideford pots. This leaves a bold picture in low relief.

The top photographs show a rounded hacksaw blade used to 'tone' an outline drawing *(top left)* and, *top right,* to clean out the whole background area. The photographs *above, right and below* show an awl used for drawing and lettering.

30

Techniques

3 Drawing with a pointed tool, followed by the use of either a riffler or rounded hack-saw blade to tone and enhance the effect, like shading on a pencil drawing.

It is essential to work with a fine body, for it is very difficult to draw good clean lines working on clays which are coarse.

Designs using these methods can be enhanced by the use of oxides applied with a brush. I use the ordinary-size Chinese brush. Smaller ones are useless as they neither hold enough liquid nor come to a good point. We are not aiming at beautiful brush strokes as in on-glaze painting (Faience), but enhancing the scratched drawing with areas of colour. It is best to explain at this stage how each oxide behaves:–

Copper (Green) This bleeds and burns away in the bisque if not applied strongly enough, but if it is applied too 'black' it becomes metallic after glazing and drips in an unsightly way down a vertical pot.

Cobalt (Blue) I prefer a pale greyish blue to the pure strong lapis-lazuli colour of neat cobalt oxide and use this recipe: iron 3 parts, manganese 2 parts, cobalt 1 part. This oxide burns in (becomes more intense) in the bisque, so use it lightly. It does not bleed or run at all.

Manganese (Brown) This is the best tempered of all the oxides. It does not bleed or alter in the bisque and remains as you painted it. Lightly applied it is a soft pinkish brown, but is a rather unattractive brown if applied heavily.

Antimony (poisonous, bright lemon yellow) This bleeds excessively and opacifies. It disappears completely in the bisque but is very strong and reacts only under the fritted glaze. Use it with a slim paint brush very sparingly in little dots or lines and not too close to your drawing outline. Because of its toxicity some potters may prefer not to use it.

The traditional English method is to enhance the work with copper oxide under a honey glaze, but elsewhere in Europe several different oxides are used (*mezza-maiolica*). I grind the black copper oxide on a glass slab with an old putty knife, adding a little water. It is then put in a

Oxides ready for polychrome painting.

china jar with a lid that acts as a palette. Copper oxide is a strange material, fearfully absorbent, so I place the jar on a larger plate. In this way I can have a stronger and a weaker mixture, both available one alongside the other.

I grind the cobalt mixture and put it in a small lidded jam jar with water. I put only a little on my palette (an old white plate) at a time, and it should be used very weak.

The manganese I grind and treat in the same way as the copper. The antimony is ground with water, and put in a tiny covered jar, using a saucer as a palette.

All the oxides rest on the inevitable plastic tray, each with its own water container and brush, and the whole apparatus is placed on newspaper, which I use to try out the tone of the oxides on my brush. All these oxides appear grey (except the antimony, which is white), and this makes them especially difficult to use, particularly when you are interrupted in your work and forget which colour was on your brush. Needless to say, a separate brush is required for each oxide if one is using several colours at the same time.

The oxides are applied fairly dry so they do not run on the more vertical sides of hollow wares, but on plaques and dishes you can treat them almost like water-colours. On the flat plates, I sometimes like to use the colour stronger, to give punch to the design, but like all the other slipware techniques it takes a long

31

The coat-of-arms of Queen Elizabeth the Queen Mother. A 16″ charger with sgraffito design, cut-out background and manganese painting, clear glaze.

time to learn just how much and how wet to use the oxides.

The cobalt, manganese and antimony only look right under a clear glaze; the copper is good under both this and the honey glaze.

The possibilities of developing sgraffito techniques are enormous. The Germans and Swiss are particularly adept at cutting, scratching and painting, nearly always under a transparent, not honey, glaze, and often trailing as well as scratching and cutting away, and painting with slips as well as oxides.

Cutting Away means sharply removing all the white engobe from around the drawing with a hack-saw blade to reveal the body colour of the pot. Dig deep enough to remove the engobe but not so much as to create hollows. Be very careful to finish with a reasonably smooth surface. Use a soft brush to clear away the residual engobe dust into a bowl. Do not blow it all over the pottery.

Writing on pots is fun. It is better to use legible 'handwriting' rather than bad calligraphy. A kind of flowing copperplate which reads easily is fairly decorative. I do not suggest using a calligraphic type nib (i.e. bamboo sharpened at an angle), or a brass nib – these are only for the dedicated letterer, who will then use the words

as decoration rather than as messages. Reading poetry takes on a new dimension as suitable phrases for inscribing jump out from the page. Limericks, doggerel, proverbs and witticisms appear on Continental and English eighteenth- and nineteenth-century pots, and with charming frequency the same concepts crop-up from separate sources independently in different languages. 'Die Pfanne ist aus Erde gemacht, wer sie zerbricht, der Häfner lacht': if you translate these inscriptions the words are more or less the same as their English equivalents.

The sgraffito technique is a wonderful illustrative medium once you have absorbed these three rules:

1 A good smooth surface to work on.
2 A leather-hard pot you can handle.
3 A finished pot with all the rough areas removed before glazing.

This last rule is the dull part of the job. When the pot is perfectly dry and ready to put in the bisque kiln, take the rounded side of a steel kidney and scrape away any surplus clay. Unfortunately in the bisque firing the rough areas seem to become more pronounced, so the whole process is repeated again, feeling each pot carefully to ensure it is absolutely smooth.

One of the pleasures of slipware pottery is its tactile quality – the soft raised areas on the trailed wares and the indentations on the sgraffito ware. The dryer you are able to work, the less the likelihood of the finished pot's being rough.

Scratching is a good technique of decorating for those who find the trailer too difficult. Working on a leather-hard pot gives a particular pleasure. It can be held in the hand in a comfortable way and if the commission is not too troublesome the drawing can be intensely satisfying. It is also helpful to work in this discipline as a contrast to the trailing discipline, which is done on the wheel in a very intense and breathless way.

Each potter can explore for himself the combination of different sgraffito techniques, whether it is drawing, painting, cutting away or inscribing.

Cheese platter 'Cote d'azur' by the author, 1985. Sgraffito and polychrome under a clear glaze. 14″ diameter.

Left **a birth plate (see page 120) and,** *above,* **'Home Sweet Home'. Both 9″ diameter; white, orange and blue slip on white engobe, under a honey glaze.**

Slip-trailed egg stand and winged cup. Seventeenth-century Staffordshire. *Fitzwilliam Museum, Cambridge.*

3 Glazes and Kilns

Now we come to the most testing part of the potter's week, the kiln firings. Everything has gone well, the engobe fits the body, the decoration is passable, the plates and jugs are turned and are all completely dry. It is time to lay all the pots out on your tables and trolleys so that you see the whole contents of the pack. Check every piece for any roughnesses, inaccurate wording, or what I call 'pockles' in the slips. These are tiny craters which, if not opened out gently with a hack-saw blade, will create little air holes which the glaze cannot penetrate. They are probably caused by using the trailers when they are nearly empty. Steel wool is excellent material for cleaning the bottoms of pots, provided you do this job in an area away from wet wares and keep all this 'dust' in a separate bowl.

Sgraffito ware needs to be carefully felt for rough areas inevitably raised by your scratching tool. Provided there is not much oxide used on the wares, this can be effectively cut off with the rounded side of a steel kidney. It is best not to handle important pieces more than absolutely necessary at this stage, especially if painted with oxides, which smudge easily, so the smoothing process can be left until after the pots are bisque fired. Make sure the holes pierced in the foot rims for hanging cords are smooth, and check all lettering for uncrossed t's and undotted i's. Sometimes it is possible to alter spelling mistakes in the sgraffito technique, such as changing an i into a c, but nothing can be done to rectify faults on slip-trailed wares.

Much of the slipware potter's output is commissioned, so do not stack inscribed plates on top of one another, particularly on oxide-painted wares, as you will get some imprint from the pigments on to the reverse of a pot.

It is important that the bisque firing should be slow. In my electric kiln I fire for three hours with ports and bung open at '50' on the Sunvic thermostat control, and then for about nine hours with everything closed overnight at '60' Sunvic. Then I finish fairly rapidly, raising the Sunvic towards maximum (100) until I reach temperature 960/980°C within an hour, then switch off. I open the bung to help cooling at 500°C, and by the following morning we are able to unpack and prepare for the glost.

No-one can instruct others in words alone on methods of firing and packing kilns, for every kiln has its own particular temperament and every potter's work is different. I can only tell you what works for me in my own kiln and with my work. The only universal rules are that the pots must be completely dry and perfectly prepared and smooth before firing.

As pyrometers are not very accurate it is wise to use pyrometric cones to check the temperature until you can be sure of the extent of any error in the pyrometer.

Glaze and glazing

As it is not only dangerous but also illegal to use lead in a raw state, most potters work with a 'safe' fritted form of lead, such as lead bisilicate or lead sesquisilicate.

After three years of trial and error I have ultimately arrived at a glaze recipe which fits the clay body and the slip, does not craze and is extremely hard wearing provided it is fired to the correct temperature. The basic recipe for my *clear* glaze is:

Lead sesquisilicate*	75
China clay	18
Flint	6

*This material is readily available in the United Kingdom from Potterycrafts, Campbell Road, Stoke-on-Trent.

For a *pale honey* glaze, one per cent of iron should be added to the above recipe, and for a *dark honey* glaze, 2 per cent of iron should be added. Potters making slipware usually require only one transparent glaze.

Add the materials to the water, and then sieve it through a 120 lawn mesh sieve to achieve a thin, batter-like consistency.

Before you begin to prepare for the glost firing, biscuited pots should be laid out on clean areas – I use clean pot boards on old tea trolleys (cheaply bought in junk shops), which can be wheeled near the glaze tubs. At this stage all the work is checked again for roughnesses, and all the sgraffito work is attacked with a steel kidney to remove the slightest ridge of raised clay, and the residual dust gently brushed away.

We proceed to stir the glaze very thoroughly with a scooping movement. If you stir the material round and round you can still leave a precipitate in the bottom of the bin. I use glaze tongs for glazing the hollow wares; this needs a bit of muscle development, as the tongs have

Using glaze tongs a mug is lifted out of the glaze bucket, shaken gently and placed on a stilt.

to be clasped tightly in the hand for a longish period. Pass the pots quickly through the glaze and place gently on the appropriate stilt, allowing plenty of room between pots. I use stilts under hollow wares for three reasons: firstly, earthenware is by its nature porous, so glazing underneath the pot is imperative; secondly, the customer needs a smooth surface

to place on his furniture; thirdly, it is (surprisingly) much easier to glaze the pots all over than to wipe off surplus material neatly. My glaze does not take kindly to a watery line at the base of a pot, which is the result of careless sponging. When removing dry glaze from the foot rim of a plate, a very crisp finish is needed, probably made with the back of a short thumbnail.

Stilts come in convenient sizes for all pots. Even the Romans used them! Do not use a stilt twice on the same side, because once the point of the stilt is blunt it will scar the pot. To remove the stilt, or its residual mark, after firing, I turn jugs and mugs upside down and give them a smart thwack with a chisel (bevel side down) and mallet. If you do the same, make sure not to make your base too thin, otherwise you will make a large hole. The foot rims of the plates are all deep enough to allow plenty of clearance for the glaze underneath, so that the plates do not stick to the kiln shelves.

Despite all the time spent in making sure pots are perfectly glazed, the earthenware potter still has a financial advantage over the stoneware expert, for his firings cost less – stoneware uses 200°C more heat-energy.

Time spent in preparation and application of the glaze is well spent, for the results are very rewarding, particularly when your customer, having admired the picture and wording on the front of the plate, turns it over and sees not only the holes for hanging his plate on the wall but also a drawing slip-trailed in white under the plate.

Do not forget to shake off any excess drops of glaze with the pot *rim down* – this obviates large globs on the base of the pot. If these do occur, fettle them gently with a knife blade when dry, before firing.

Flat wares should be glazed in a large open container (I use a galvanized horse feeder, 24 inches in diameter, 8 inches high). With two fingers on either side of the plate, pass this through the glaze. Lay the glazed pot down on a pristine surface. Unlike the jugs and mugs described above, flat ware should have its foot rim cleaned of glaze. This is best done with the fingers, making a small bevel either side. Do not

In my pottery, each glaze has its own 'touch-up kit' – a mug and a brush on a very small plastic tray – and these kits I place near the kiln. With the tip of a Chinese brush I drop little fresh blobs of glaze on to the bald areas where either my fingers have held the plate or I have knocked off the glaze while cleaning the foot. It is no good brushing on the glaze as it will not be thick or even enough for a convincing repair.

Packing the kiln and firing

When you pack the kiln do not place two rows of shelves exactly opposite each other. Stagger the pack and try, if possible, to keep hollow wares alternating with flat wares; this allows a free flow of heat. Pack as close as possible within the shelves for economy.

A plate is passed through well-stirred glaze and shaken to remove any drops. The glaze is cleaned off the foot rim with the fingers, *below*.

The packing of a glost kiln is always a tricky business, and the kiln must be kept 'open' in places; by this I mean that tallish hollow wares should be placed opposite shelves of flat wares. All kilns have their own personality, even electric ones. My particular kiln is cool at the top, and this area is useful for packing clear glaze pots that are either many-coloured (polychrome) or decorated with cobalt. If these mugs or bowls are placed in hotter areas the slip is inclined to burn out slightly and become faintly blotchy-looking in appearance.

I always use castellated props between shelves as these allow one greater flexibility, and if you do not drop them too often they will last for years. I allow one $1\frac{1}{2}$ inch and one 1 inch prop between flat plates, and always one inch of space above hollow wares.

Carefully place a pyrometric cone (supported by clay) on a small piece of kiln shelf with a nite-light behind for viewing through the spy hole. Do not forget to remove the nite-light. We used to use a torch until once we forgot to remove it!

Here is the simple pattern of the glost firing of my Cromartie kiln for my own work:

forget to stir the glaze again if you are called to the telephone.

The glaze formula on page 35 makes a wonderfully good-tempered glaze; it does not run if fired to the correct temperature, and it is also easy to work with at the pre-firing stage. We do not sponge foot rims until just before placing the pots in the kiln.

on at 22.00 – (time switch) set Sunvic at 60
     07.00 – reading approximately 900°C, 70 Sunvic
     08.00 – reading approximately 1000°C, 80 Sunvic

09.30 – reading approximately 1050°C, soak one hour using your control mechanism at this temperature. At this stage the Orton standard pyrometric cone LRB 05 should be well arched.

10.30 – switch off.

For any other kiln these timings are irrelevant. You must carefully control your own schedule, just as every potter has to find his own way of packing his kiln. For the slipware potter, where perhaps the major part of his output is commissioned work entailing a great deal of thoughtful and elaborate decoration, the pattern of firing is absolutely vital, as one is not relying on haphazard or even controlled effects achieved by high temperature or reduction. The aim is to get a simple rise of temperature over the right period of time and to arrive exactly at 1040°C–1050°C when it is convenient to you in your working day, and then to hold your kiln at this temperature for one hour.

Most electric kilns nowadays are, or can be, equipped with time clocks and cut-out mechanisms, and I suggest that you spend some money on a fail-safe device. I have three times lost the entire contents and interior of a kiln through my assistant's misunderstanding of the 24-hour clock, and it is easy to be involved in some unforeseen crisis which causes you to leave the kiln unattended. The *pye-ether* magical switch will simply hold the temperature at whatever degree your experience tells you to set it, and your time switch will turn the kiln off before any damage is done.

Kilns

The earthenware potter is lucky. He can buy an electric kiln with a maximum temperature below that required for stoneware. This is cheaper than a high-firing kiln, and the most expensive firing time (the long pull to final temperature) is briefer and lower. Electric kilns are best for earthenware. Do not bother with gas or oil. Reducing atmospheres often cloud your decorative line. It is also best to stick to a straightforward, old fashioned, front-loading kiln, placed at exactly the right height on a stand. If you are very clever you have large wheels fitted to the legs, which make moving, when and if it happens, a cheerful as opposed to a traumatic experience.

Having to change a kiln means a break in the work pattern. It may take three months to get used to the new beast and to achieve the correct firings. This can mean an important loss of production and income.

There are ceramic-fibre top-loading kilns which are cheap and economic to run, but these are not for the serious slipware potter, who needs his kiln placed at a comfortable height with the whole area visible all the time for ease of packing – particularly where stilts are used.

Remember your kiln is also your heating/drying mechanism in the workshop, and your work should be planned to fill it with appropriate-sized wares each week. Do not choose too small a kiln, and certainly not a very large one – for what you need is a quick turnover, both for your pleasure and your customers' satisfaction. The aim should be to complete individual orders in three weeks.

In a small workshop things will get very dry during firings so, if possible, try to arrange a separate small room for keeping clay and holding back freshly decorated work, or pots that you do not have time to deal with immediately.

The interior size of the kiln must suit your own work, not an abstract formula. My 'bread and butter line' is a range of 9 and 12 inch plates, with sometimes 18 inch chargers. It is very important for me to be able to fit two 9 inch plates side by side on a shelf, and comfortably allow for a 14 inch diameter platter on another shelf. The kiln supplier will cut shelves to your specifications, and it is very useful to have at least one variant on the standard size; for example, instead of two 12 × 18 inch shelves, have one 10 × 18 inch and its pair 14 × 18.

A new kiln is an expensive – probably your most expensive – purchase, and you cannot afford to make mistakes. Choose a kiln from a maker with a good service record. If you buy a second-hand kiln it is best to buy it from the maker, to whom you can complain if necessary.

Part 2 The Heritage

Two-handled cup. Wrotham, 6″ high.

4 English slip-trailed wares

Metropolitan tyg, sixteenth century. 6″ high. White slip trailed over an orange body. Honey glaze. *Museum of London.*

Wrotham and Metropolitan wares

The earliest known slip-trailed wares in England were made at Wrotham in Kent (1612–1739), east of Sevenoaks and close to the Pilgrims' Way. There are some one hundred of these pots extant, many dated and with initials. Generally speaking, the forms are loving cups, candlesticks and puzzle jugs, most of the pots having looped handles ornamented with contrasting coils of clay and thickly slipped and embossed pads of clay.

It is interesting to see that this work was fired on 'shoulders', as opposed to stilts, to prevent the glaze sticking to the kiln shelves or saggars. By examining the pots in the Museum of London it is evident that this was the case. This is the only instance I have ever seen of this type of kiln furniture being used under slipwares in the seventeenth century or later.

Of all the Wrotham wares, the form that I like best is a large belly-shaped cup 6 inches high, with two handles positioned on the one side. It is easy to imagine much quaffing of ale and rumbustuous talk around the smoking hearth. These vessels were used only on Christmas Eve in Derby and Staffordshire – this might account for the excellent condition of many 'tygs' (drinking vessels) found in the present-day museums.

The style of decoration of these pots may be derived from the German bellarmines, the classic stoneware bottles impressed with the

English slip-trailed wares

'greybeard' mask, but I always find it difficult to substantiate these hypotheses. Often new ways of decoration emerge independently as one experiments with the medium. Alternating twists of red and white clay adorn the surface of pulled handles, knobs sit on top of the handles, the initials of the potters and the date are often impressed into a white pad of thick slip on the pots. The last potter working in Wrotham was one Thomas Ifield, and his initials appear on several of the drinking vessels.

I see the rumbustuous humour of the post-fifteenth century era being perfectly encapsulated in the puzzle jug, a jug made frequently with open work cut into the neck, the liquid being carried up through the pierced handle to a hollow coil on the top of the neck. This had several outlets, one of which was the sucking spout. The puzzle tygs are unusual, as they have a domed false bottom and the ale rises up through one of the pierced handles to be drunk through a small nipple. These jugs and tygs occur in all European countries of this and later periods. The Hungarian strictly functional water pitcher has a nipple on its handle, through which the water is drunk. As these Hungarian forms are very early, one wonders if they had an influence on the humorous English jug of the sixteenth and later centuries.

The Wrotham pots are certainly unique, and the mass of thickly applied decoration gives them an endearing quality. Although at first sight they may appear ugly, like so much slipware it is worth studying them to appreciate the intricacy of the skills involved in making these historic pieces.

The other early pottery site making decorated wares, named by Sir Augustus Franks as *Metropolitan wares*, was Harlow in Essex where a brown boulder clay of glacial origin was dug. It had little admixture of chalk and other rocks and was very plastic. To complete the potters' needs, brushwood and water were also available in abundance in the district and the whole of Harlow Common was pitted with depressions of clay pits before ploughing in World War I.

Parish Registers show that there was much inter-marrying in the early seventeenth century between three of the main pottery families, the

A Wrotham candlestick dated 1668, 11″ high, attributed to George Richardson.
Below Metropolitan ware, seventeenth century.

40

English slip-trailed wares

most important of whom were the Wrights. The first John Wright, 1636, in his will left to his son 'all my workhouse, potting bords and wheels and all working tools and things belonging to the trade of a potter, 2 sheds, rest of the yard. Al my Bush Fayre stuff, poles, stratchers, bordes, plankes, al the borde nayled on and about the cupp clay bynn.'

Early records of this type are helpful in forming a picture of the potters' working conditions as none of the wood or iron artefacts appear to have survived the centuries, although some pots have.

In the first part of the seventeenth century, a road was built between Newcastle and London via Harlow. This probably accounts for the large amount of this ware being found in the City of London. Metropolitan pots were all decorated with a white or pale orange slip on to the body of the pot with strong simple triangular or fir tree motifs.

During the building of Harlow New Town, the sites of small potteries were discovered at Potter Street, a village two miles south of Harlow crossroads, and part of the straggling Latton parish. Bulldozers levelling the ground destroyed much of the evidence, but many coarse domestic wares were found, such as pitchers with one or two handles and lip, large vessels 12 inches high for storing liquid, with bungs and decorated with grooving or white brushed slip; oval dishes with lip and handle; black glazed tygs; large mixing or washing bowls 6 inches high and 16 inches in diameter; candlesticks and a puzzle jug. Many of these pots are unglazed, but some have a little glaze in the base of the pots or on the shoulder and some are decorated with strong brush strokes of white slip.

Oval fish 'cookers' were found and large wash basins, as well as black glazed tygs. These needed more sophisticated kiln furniture to prevent them sticking to the shelves; and sure enough rings, and rings with spikes, were found as well as clay trivets. It is interesting that the latter form – the stilt – has not been improved upon over the succeeding centuries, except that now they are commercially manufactured to a finer specification. Saggars, also found on the

Jonathan Snell slip trailing a salt kit using a horn.

site, were used to protect the glazed Metropolitan ware such as the puzzle jugs from the flames. A good example of such a jug can be seen in the Fitzwilliam Museum, Cambridge, dated 1632.

I think it is important to emphasise the fine quality of the slip-trailed decoration on the Metropolitan wares: one can only speculate on the tool used. It was either a pouring cup with quill attached or a horn. I used to think the horn was the principal tool but since I have been sporadically using one myself I have found it has a very short life. The horn becomes so dry and cracked with the use of clay slip and in the atmosphere of the pottery. The only way you can restore horn is by feeding it: that is, soaking it in oil, and this would then make it unusable, causing a 'resist' and completely spoiling the trailing and subsequent glazing.*

On many country slipwares, such as salt kits and jugs and some bowls, the vessel is held with the left hand inside and the slip poured from the trailer on to the outside of an upside-down pot.

*Since writing this I have discovered that if the horn is highly polished, this cracking does not occur so readily.

41

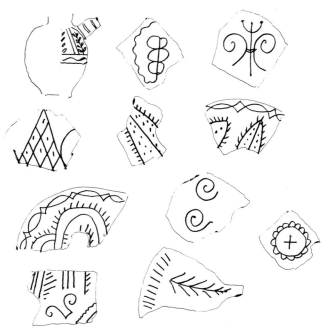

Motifs from Metropolitan wares on sherds from a kiln site in Harlow. *c.* 1627.

This demands a lot of dexterity but it does make for fluidity in the patterning, and it is easy to put the pot down neatly on a board afterwards. With the Metropolitan jugs, where so much lettering is used, the problem is different and the pots would have to be held the right way up, but still with the hand inside. The trailing tool was a *pouring* tool. Dr Plot, in his *History of Staffordshire 1667*, described this as a 'bucket'. This was made of clay, having a large opening at the top through which it was filled, and a small hole in the front into which a goose quill was inserted. It was not like our modern trailers, where we extrude the clay and can therefore place the pot to be decorated on its bat on a banding wheel at a convenient height. I recommend present-day decorators to attempt the pouring method on hollow wares: if nothing else, it will prove to them how difficult a task it is.

I feel that Metropolitan ware is generally underestimated. Wherever slip-trailed decoration is employed without the help of infilling, an extra degree of skill is required. Although the motifs on this ware appear limited, the sureness and skill of the execution is apparent. The forms are also pleasant: baluster-

shaped unlipped jugs and simple tygs. Even the chamber pots are elegant. As their diameter (7 inch approximately) is so small, it is probable that they were piss-pots. One must assume that no stool pots have survived.

Many of these wares show marks of burning and some believe this to indicate that they were affected by the Great Fire of London in 1660.

Unlike much of the Toft ware, which was Royalist in sympathy (see pages 43, 45), the inscriptions on Metropolitan ware from Harlow were mostly Puritan in character. Charles Lomax says all showy or gaudy ware would have been classed as 'ungodly'. Lomax was one of the early admirers of English seventeenth-century slipwares: he wrote a charming book, lavishly illustrated with sepia photos, published in London in 1884. The frontispiece to the book shows the bearded patriarch bearing on his face an expression of ineffable pleasure as he holds in his hands the famous Royal Oak charger by Thomas Toft. Unfortunately this valuable collection of pots was destroyed by fire, but his informative book survived and helped to encourage interest in what was, at that time, a largely unregarded art.

Some examples of inscriptions on Metropolitan ware are: 'Fast and Preay', 'Amend they life and sin no more', 'Feare God Ever', and strangely enough 'Honor thy King'. And on a chamber pot: 'Break me not I pray in your hast for I to you will give distast'.

OBEAY THE KING
REMEMBER FHY END FRVES
OBEAY GODS WOVRD
HEL9 LORD FOR GOD
AND GOD LS MEN DO
BE MERK AND W!2

Inscriptions from Metropolitan wares.

42

William Talor. Coronation charger, seventeenth-century Staffordshire, 18″ diameter.
Fitzwilliam Museum, Cambridge.

Staffordshire

The bulk of slip-trailed wares in the seventeenth century was produced in Staffordshire, many kinds of clay being freely available, including fire clay for the saggars. Lead ore could be procured five miles from Burslem and sold for six or seven shillings (35 pence, or 50 cents) per ton. At an earlier date, lead was also found in Derby, melted by wood and coal fires on hillsites in places called 'hearths and boles'.

When we look at nineteenth-century prints of Stoke-on-Trent it is difficult to imagine the vast areas of woodland that then were so close. In 1656, Needwood Forest covered 9229 acres, and in the eighteenth century this woodland carried 20,000 head of deer. The River Trent provided the transport, the ports of Chester and Liverpool were not far away, and in 1766 Josiah Wedgwood cut the first clod of the Trent & Mersey Canal. This canal, allied to the establishment of the railways around 1850, contributed to the demise of the more rustic potteries.

There are many references in the seventeenth-century Court Rolls to the nuisances caused by

Detail from a large dish by Ralph Toft, *c.* 1680, in the County Museum, Dorchester.

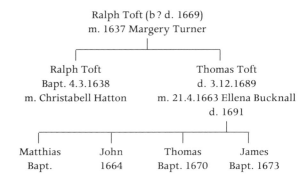

Ralph Toft (b ? d. 1669)
m. 1637 Margery Turner

Ralph Toft
Bapt. 4.3.1638
m. Christabell Hatton

Thomas Toft
d. 3.12.1689
m. 21.4.1663 Ellena Bucknall
d. 1691

Matthias
Bapt.

John
1664

Thomas
Bapt. 1670

James
Bapt. 1673

Toft are known and all except three are dishes between 17 and 22 inches in diameter. They are wheel-thrown, but I am inclined to believe that Toft did only the decorating, not the throwing. None of the trailing is banded on the wheel, and it would have been inconvenient for the throwing and decorating to be done by the same man. One can see this same system at work now in rural potteries in Europe, where different rooms with cleaner conditions and a better light source are used for decoration.

potters as they dug indiscriminately for their clay, undermining the highways and endangering lives.

The emergence of a particular kind of elaborately decorated earthenware at this period appears surprising, and it is difficult to define the sources of inspiration. We know of the Roman Castor ware with its white patterns trailed skilfully on to a black body, and of bowls from Holland decorated with cockerels in slip. The tin-glazed Delft wares, with their formal portraits of Kings and Queens, are the nearest to the emergent Staffordshire style, but it is difficult to see how any of this work could have been available to Staffordshire's most famous potter, Thomas Toft.

Sadly, nothing is known of his life other than genealogical facts collected from parish registers and the hearth tax roll for Stanley, near Leek, except that his was a Catholic family with strong Royalist leanings. Thirty-four pieces by Thomas

A Roman vessel with white slip trailing on a black body, and applied painted heads, from Trier.

The royal coat-of-arms by Thomas Toft, 20½" diameter, 1871, in the Grosvenor Museum, Chester. It is known as the Heues plate, following the inscription.

In Toft's work the drawing of the designs was done in a dark brown slip (red clay coloured with manganese), and then infilled with either red or orange slip, the latter being made of a mixture of white and red clay. Nearly all these outlines were jewelled with minute dots of white slip, this being all the more remarkable as the engobe was poured from a clay vessel or cow-horn elongated with a goose quill, a seemingly impossible task when one considers the fine line achieved over such a large area of drawing. It needed a very free-running slip to pass through this narrow tube without means of extruding.

All these wares were thrown in a very pale body, and, when decorated, were once-fired after having a lead glaze poured over them. This sequence of events is supported by the fact that no biscuited sherds have been found in the various Stoke excavations.

Owl and owlets on a moulded dish, 16¼"
diameter, Staffordshire ware, *c.* 1730.

The glazing on these Toft dishes is so
excellent that I am inclined to believe that a
satisfactory method of suspension was achieved
at this earlier period, using a small proportion
of slurry in the lead/water mix.* Flint would not
have been introduced into the glaze until the
time of Thomas Astbury in the late seventeenth
century. There is a contention that iron was not
added to this honey glaze, and the colour was
achieved through the impurities in the lead itself
and, perhaps, with the addition of red clay
slurry. But, as already mentioned, most if not all
of the Toft plates are thrown in a white body.
To my knowledge there is only one Staffordshire
pot extant, in the Manchester Museum (Greg
Collection), with a truly clear glaze. It is a large

seventeenth-century caudle or bragget pot with
two handles and unusual heart decoration.
There is a lot of bleed from the manganese in the
black slip and the whole effect is unique and
very attractive (see page 68).

All the Staffordshire work that has survived
from the seventeenth century was made for
presentation and is remarkable for the quality of
the drawing, the design and liveliness of
imagination. None of the dishes by other named
potters, such as Ralph Simpson, William Talor,
John Wright, James Johnson, and Toft's three
working sons (Matthias probably died young)
has the wonderful skill of Thomas Toft senior,
but they all have a liveliness and naïve charm.
It is easy for some experts to underestimate the
technical skills involved : many people talk
about this as 'crude work'. Those who have
handled a modern slip-trailer feel very humble
when they confront the work of the
seventeenth-century potter who poured his
designs from a 'bucket' or cow-horn, and
achieved with this imperfect tool such vigorous
results. Although seventeenth-century slipware
was undervalued until recent years it is now
fetching high prices in the Art House auction
rooms.

It is always fascinating to speculate on the
design sources, particularly as the bulk of
thrown dishes are decorated with Royalist

*According to Miss Meteyard, who wrote a fascinating life of
Josiah Wedgwood, published in 1787, fluid glazes were
introduced only in 1750. Her book is of particular interest
because she was writing about a period almost contemporary
with her own. The book has a certain poignancy : she makes us
re-live the life in the potteries as it was then, recalling the pall
of smoke over the five towns and the sound of horses' hooves
on the rough cobbles. Above all, there is the picture of Josiah
Wedgwood, the potter, the artist and the politician, seen against
this prosperous but satanic background.

English slip-trailed wares

subjects and have political overtones. Richard Gough, writing in his *History of Myddle* (1620), states: 'All men were troubled by the outrages and pilferings of soldiers of bothe parties seeing their goodes and horses taken away, some died of broken heart.' In addition, there were 'emblem books' (pattern books) in existence at this period, and many similarities can be found between embroidery subjects, the Staffordshire slip-trailed and the imported Delft wares.

As well as the dishes, many other forms from other Staffordshire potteries have survived, including:

owl jugs (see page 28)
cradles, which were often as long as 12 inches and were given as fertility symbols to young married couples
tobacco jars
globular jugs, inspired by the German 'Westerwald' shapes
egg stands
small impress-moulded dishes, approximately 7 inches in diameter, often decorated with stags and royal emblems
candlesticks
cruets
puzzle jugs
small cups, often with feathered decoration

Slip trailed cradle with press-moulded decoration. Staffordshire, 1673.

Posset pots (see page 11) had an unusual shape, with a spout emerging from the base of the pot as well as having two handles and a lid. Some even had, contained under the knob, a little bowl to hold the spices used. 'Possets' were the

A moulded dish by William Bird. Staffordshire, *c.* 1751. With slip trailed decoration near the rim, the incised mould alongside is made of buff clay. *Manchester City Art Gallery.*

stand-by of the sick room for almost two centuries. Most cookery books of the seventeenth and eighteenth centuries included recipes for making them: milk or cream was curdled with ale, wine or brandy to which spices were added. The favourite recipe was one which was called the 'carduus posset', since it was made with the 'blessed thistle', *carduus benedictus*. The resulting mixture, consisting of

Slip trailed Dutch oven, eighteenth-century Staffordshire.

47

Impress-moulded dish with two gloves as the central motif. Possibly by Samuel Malkin, eighteenth century. *Manchester City Art Gallery.*

curds and whey, was then separated by pouring off the whey through the spout of the pot – this was the posset for drinking – and the remaining curd was eaten. When made with a fortified wine spiced and sugared, the posset gave great comfort to the sufferer from a chill or fever. Elizabeth David, writing in the 1980s, quotes from an earlier source where it is mentioned the cow was milked directly into the pot containing spiced wine and sugar, and as the milk was warm, the posset immediately separated into curds and whey.

The inscription on many of the pots is 'The best is not too good for you.' Posset pots were made in different sizes, ranging from a half-pint to almost four pints. The larger sizes provided ample opportunity for elaborate forms of decoration. They were made both in lead-glazed earthenware and in tin glaze.

'Caudle' or 'bragget' pots were used for a spiced, warm ale drink, what we would now call mulled ale. There are many silver caudle pots of this period extant, so it is reasonable to assume

the drink could not have been too hot on serving.

It is important to remember that the pots that have survived 300 years were treasured family possessions and used only on ritual occasions, so that our picture of the pots in daily use at that period must necessarily be imperfect.

In earlier times, pewter, horn and wood were in general use for drinking vessels. The discovery of coffee, tea and chocolate – hot drinks – must have made glazed clay drinking vessels doubly welcome. At this same period (1660s), tin-glazed ware was being imported from Holland, particularly into East Anglia. A Dutch Fair was held annually at Yarmouth and houses in that area would have been full of Dutch pots. This 'Delftware', as it came to be called, was of superior whiteness owing to the soft tin glaze, and would have gradually superseded the lead-glazed Staffordshire decorative pots before the advent of the factory-made 'pearl' wares.

I have not written at greater length about the

mainstream of slip-decorated wares in England between the seventeenth and nineteenth centuries, because the English slipwares are widely known and well documented (see bibliography). Famous collections in England can easily be visited for study: the Glaisher Collection at the Fitzwilliam Museum in Cambridge, the Greg Collection at Manchester City Art Gallery, and the Ceramic Collection at the City Museum & Art Gallery in Hanley, Stoke-on-Trent, the Victoria & Albert English ceramic collection and the British Museum slipware collection. For those who live in or visit the USA, there is the Burnap Collection at the Nelson Gallery at the Atkins Museum in Kansas City, Missouri.

Moulded dishes, formerly attributed to Derbyshire. *Above* **hunting scene with hounds and the fox, and,** *below,* **a stag, dated 1736.** *Manchester City Art Gallery.*

Derbyshire

The two eighteenth-century moulded dishes illustrated on this page are particularly lively and their theme, the hunting scene, is the only one appearing on English pottery that has much affinity with continental wares. The sureness of execution of the decoration on both dishes shows that there must have been many pots decorated in this series. By the eighteenth century many plates were moulded, while thrown dishes were standard to the end of the seventeenth century, except for a group of little impress-moulded dishes coming from Staffordshire in the 1650s. Curiously enough, many of the latter had stag decorations as well as royal emblems. The clay on these was very thin, as it needed to be pressed well into the mould to receive the embossed patterns.

Many articles were formerly attributed to Ticknall (1650–1880s), where lead was extensively mined ('Earthen vessels, potts and pancions at Ticknall and carried all East England thru . . .'). The last pottery closed in the 1880s. However, the attribution is now in dispute.

I particularly like an attractive group of wares which must have come from the hand of one potter. On these a very lively and broad line is scratched through the black slip to reveal the white pot underneath. A stag was often the principal motif, as was the tulip. The forms are fairly typical of the period except that the small

straight-sided mugs are before their time. These can be found in the City Museum, Hanley, and the Victoria & Albert Museum, South Kensington, London, where it is rewarding to study the effects of scratching through black to white, a technique seldom used in Britain.

Yorkshire

There is no evidence yet of seventeenth-century Yorkshire pottery, although pottery was a thriving industry in the eighteenth century with most of the work being redwares and functional pots for the local market, such as pancheons, 'barm pots', bread and ham pots and stew pots.

It is interesting to quote William Cobbett who, writing in *Rural Rides* (1821) stated :

> When fairs were very frequent . . . shops were not needed. A manufacturer of shoes, of stockings, of hats, of almost anything that man wanted, could manufacture at home in an obscure hamlet, with cheap house rents, good air and plenty of room. He need pay no heavy rent for a shop and no disadvantages from a confined situation, and then by attending five or six fairs a year he sold the work of his hands unloaded with a heavy expense attending the keeping of a shop.

In the eighteenth century many small potteries made slipwares in the Halifax region, as there was excellent coal, fire clay and pot clay available. The prosperous wool towns of Yearsly, Howcans and Midhope were also within carting distance, as markets.

Burton in Lonsdale 1740–1944
In this small village in the nineteenth century there were at least three or four working potteries, many of them with a family history of three generations of potters.

Mr Percy Bateson of the Waterside Pottery is a healthy young man of 92 who has almost total recall of his working life. He tells me that two kinds of clay were available in Burton – stoneware and a red earthenware – but a local ball-clay was bought in for the white slip. Twenty tons of stoneware clay were used per week, with 250 gallons of water each day.

Mr Bateson entered the family business in 1906 at the age of thirteen, and he rapidly learnt to throw eighty-five bottles per day. There was a ball-boy for the throwers, but he often had to be away on other jobs so the thrower occasionally had to hump his own clay and carry the pot board. The bottles were stoneware 'liquid containers' which were impressed with the customer's name in metal type and sold in bulk, principally for alcoholic liquor. When the clay was weighed for the bottles, the measure was one Accrington brick plus a small piece of clay (about 12 lbs). Of course, many sizes were made, but the brick was always the main weight plus the variable lump of clay. These bottles were twice-fired in one of two kilns.

Mr Bateson recalls that the day for the workmen started at 6 am, with a break for breakfast at 8 o'clock and another break for lunch. They worked until 5 pm. In the dark mornings and evenings they lit the work areas by candlelight and crude oil lamps made by themselves. Burton in Lonsdale was the first Yorkshire village to receive electricity in 1920.

1919 was a prosperous year, with as many as thirty-two men employed making the stoneware bottles, which were taken by cart pulled by shire horses to Ingleton station; from here they were transported by train to Liverpool and thence to Ireland, Guinness being the principal customer, their bottles being used for bottling stout.

Three kilns were fired every week for thirteen weeks to a temperature of 1280°. Each kiln held 1,200 bottles using twelve tons of clay. Mr Bateson said that earthenware pots were made principally for pleasure in his family's concern and were slip decorated. Settle Rural

Inkwell and candleholder, Burton in Lonsdale, *c.* **1890. The candle was fixed in the 'spout'.**

'A Pedler's Basket', white slip trailed on a red body. A marriage gift from Burton in Lonsdale, 1866. 8″ high.

Life Museum contains about twenty pots, many of them inscribed with the Bateson name. They are principally hen and chicken tiered money boxes with many looped handles, bird whistles and a thrown cradle 6 inches long decorated with small white balls of clay pressed along the rim. There is both agate and marbled ware, including a magnificent 8 inch long moulded lion. All these pots have a rich honey glaze. There is also an unusual candlestick/inkwell combined with marbled slip under the Burton honey glaze.

A finely potted puzzle jug, 6 inches high, bears the inscription:

Gentlemen now try your skill
I'll bold you sixpence if you will
That you don't drink.
Unless you spill.

Tobacco jars seem a very common item of nineteenth century slipware and one from Burton in Lonsdale inscribed 'J Atkinson', has under the name a nice pattern in white slip trail and a pair of crossed clay pipes on the reverse side.

Ingleton coal-mine closed in the 1930s, and all the Burton in Lonsdale potteries had ceased operating by 1944 – a sad story. But Mr Bateson himself went on to teach at the Central School of Art in London, passing on his throwing skills. He worked under Dora Billington, who much admired him. Thus a whole generation of notable modern potters learnt their skills and a feel for pottery from Percy Bateson.

None of the old bottles are present in Mr and Mrs Bateson's house today, as 'we thought nothing of them', but some are to be seen in the newly opened Settle Rural Life Museum along with a few excellent stoneware pub barrels, sprigged and impressed. The slipwares were obviously much treasured possessions of local families, in particular the money boxes, many of which have survived in excellent condition despite all the applied clay hens and looped handles which would have made them particularly liable to breakage.

Baggaley Pottery, Greater Bridge, Burton was founded in the 1750s and had a long tradition

Mr Bateson's old family money box, *c.* 1870.

51

of making functional pots. There is an excellent knife pot in the Yorkshire Museum dated 1797, one of the few pieces still extant. This pottery, like so many others, closed finally in 1945.

Town End Pottery, also in Burton, produced brown and black wares, principally domestic pottery, with little decoration. It closed in the 1920s.

Jonathan Catherall started one of the potteries in this area at *Keelham*. He was related to the famous Catherall of the Buckley Potteries in Clwyd, North Wales.

Halifax

There were approximately ten potteries flourishing in the Halifax area in the eighteenth century, of which Denholme was one of the most interesting. Under the ownership of Nicholas Taylor in the nineteenth century it produced finely potted and decorated slipwares.

A pottery in Howcans was started in 1775 by the Halliday family, and they made some nicely decorated slipwares, many of which can be seen in the Yorkshire Museum. This pottery closed earlier than most, in 1889.

Soil Hill is perhaps the most famous of all the Yorkshire potteries. Catherall moved here from Keelham, and after his death in 1807 his grandson Samuel made some fine slipwares until his own death in 1887. It then became an unsuccessful chicken farm until it was bought by John Kitson, who worked it until his death when it was sold by his widow to Isaac Button in 1897. A film of this fine craftsman at work has guaranteed the survival of his reputation. Buttons' son – the last of the Halifax potters – retired in 1964.

Littlethorpe, near Ripon in Yorkshire, was opened in the early 1830s by James Foxton and Company. In the beginning of the twentieth century the works were sold to a Mr Richardson. The speciality of this pottery was the bigware, in particular horticultural pots thrown by Albert Kitson, who was possibly the best bigware thrower in England. The pottery was sold again in 1922 to George Curtis, a former trainee clayboy. His son still carries on making

principally plant pots, strawberry pots, garden urns, etc. The clay, which is dug, pugged and thrown on the wheel directly without weathering, is particularly good for outdoor work because of its open texture.

Although these Yorkshire potteries had all the advantages of coal, local fireclay and potclay, as soon as the transport facilities improved and smart factory wares from Staffordshire arrived in the area, trade started to decline. Competition was to drive out the rustic potter, and with this came the demise of slipware, which provided the light relief and often the social commentary in work-a-day potteries which once formed part of the fabric in an industrialising society.

Two-handled drinking vessel, slip trailed BWH 1817, from Halifax.

Chimney
bird-whistle, late
eighteenth century. 9″ high.

5 The demise of the rural potteries

The history of the Yorkshire potteries represents a typical picture of the state of the pottery trade from the eighteenth to the twentieth century.

Initially, strong and necessary domestic wares were made for a community that was ill-served by communications. The highways were sparse and there was no access to water transport; most of the conveying of news, gossip and trade was by pedlars, carriers and the stewards who often travelled in stages from the North and Midlands, through the country and into the city of London carrying out their masters' business. They would have brought back with them tales of life and society fashions as well as patterns for embroidery, wall coverings, and furniture.

The arrival of the railway, with stations situated away from the centre of towns, while improving communications spelt death to that wonderful theatrical scene, the arrival of the stage coach. All the inhabitants would turn out,

not only to greet the travellers but to sell hot pies, baskets, toys, pamphlets. It must have been a scene of intense bustle, noise and liveliness, forming a major entertainment. On market days travellers would have seen pots on display and perhaps bought some – a barm pot, maybe, or some bird whistles for the children.

Much of the local trade was drawn away by the railway and at this same period, in the nineteenth century, mechanisation and mass production got under way in Staffordshire. New machinery was invented for pugging and mixing the clay; Plaster of Paris was used for mould making; jigger and jolleying techniques were now in use to simplify large production runs of cups, bowls and plates. All these changes contributed to the slow run-down of many country potteries, culminating in World War I when the younger men went into the army and those who returned in 1918 found many of the potteries had closed, being unable to continue operating with so little labour. For the first time even the women were working in munitions factories and other establishments to further the war effort. Fuel was also in short supply, most of it being needed for more vital industry.

During the 1920s there was a desperate attempt by the rural potter to produce 'Art Wares', as the local people no longer needed the simple, functional earthenware pots. Few of these potters had any art training, as is abundantly obvious in the sometimes grotesque efforts at vases and plant pots, heavily decorated with slips and sgraffito, and applied and embossed clay ornament. Sometimes pots were advertized as being 'available for decoration', and the local parson or ladies could decorate them *in situ* and then either have them fired or take them home to brush sophisticated patterns on the ware with oil paints.

Alongside the disasters of war, the industrial revolution and the arrival of the railway, there was a further threat to the craftsman: the change and development in methods of cooking. In the seventeenth century he would have been making strong vessels designed for use on the open fire. Then came the iron kitchen-range where the three-legged piggins and round-

53

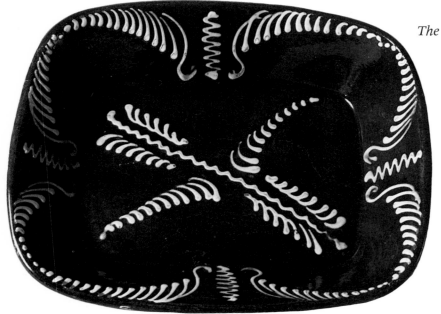

An early nineteenth-century Yorkshire moulded baking dish, 16 × 18″, with white slip trailed on a dark brown clay body.

bottomed cooking pots made for the open hearth were useless. Iron saucepans and kettles were in demand, although the earthenware baking dishes were still welcome. In fact these handsome, moulded brown dishes, some with a central division for two types of food, were made (principally in the Newcastle area) until World War II (see above).

By the late 1920s, gas cookers were coming into general use and the iron pots were replaced by aluminium, and pottery baking dishes by enamel or pyrex glass ware. This period also saw the birth of the country cottage or second home for the middle classes, and for the first time the lady of the house did a little of her own cooking. Small 'convenient' kitchens were created and a rustic atmosphere, a sort of miniature Versailles, was enjoyed. This, fortunately, gave a little respite to the village potter, and his cider jars and water pitchers were in demand. Earthenware pots for bunches of wild flowers stood on the window sill; artistic basket shapes with handles were also made to hold cowslips and primroses. Plant pots and posy rings, dog bowls and cream jugs were welcome additions to the country cottage. Butter dishes and milk bottle covers were produced out of unglazed earthenware to keep the food cool. Then the arrival of the refrigerator killed this enterprising trade. By the 1930s there was a regular import

to England of excellent gratin dishes and casseroles from Vallauris in France, the same traditional forms that are sold now in fashionable cook-shops.

Some few potteries limped on until the 1940s, finally closing down during the war, while those that did survive did so by maintaining flexibility. For instance, Wattisfield pottery in Suffolk sold their quarry land for cash, bought buff clay from Staffordshire and mass-produced moulded and slip-cast wares for large London stores, covered in bright industrial glazes.

Brannams in Barnstaple, at the turn of the century, made Art Nouveau shapes for Liberty's in London, in a strong dark-blue glaze. and developed every sort of form using slips in extraordinary ways (see facing page). But with the arrival of 'studio pottery' and the 'one-offs' produced by Bernard Leach and his followers, Brannams sensibly settled for a small range of traditional forms, different sizes of pitcher, bowl, casserole and bread crock, with either a white or black slip inside and on the rim. Alongside this excellent work (all mechanically made) they now produce jigger and jolleyed flower-pots in all sizes, which are absorbed by the thousand in garden centres and stores in the south of England. They also sell the plastic Fremington clay to potters such as Alan Caiger-Smith, and myself.

Salt kit from Wetheriggs Pottery, Penrith, 1953. White slip on brown body under a clear glaze. 8″ high.

George Curtis at Ripon in Yorkshire also produces strawberry pots and large garden pots from his own good red clay, all hand-thrown. Although most plants are now sold in plastic pots for convenience, nearly everyone wishes to transplant them into good red clay pots which not only please the eye but please the plant.

The demise of the rural potteries

The Weatheriggs pottery at Penrith in Cumbria has survived the economic storm by not only producing trailed slipwares in traditional shapes, such as the salt kit, but by turning part of the old pottery into a museum with the horse pug-mill and other old machinery. Westmorland is a tourist area and this forms an excellent educative attraction alongside the working pottery, which also produces a good range of leaflets and informative material – an invaluable source of future income, as this information is passed on to friends and relatives.

Collecting the work from some of the old country potteries such as Dicker in Sussex, one sees the sad decline in their vitality, as their forms become weak, straining often after some artistic and 'voluble' effect. Demand for their former rustic work had ceased.

The South Devon potteries were able to continue producing their rustic wares much later than many other workshops because they included 'sayings' on their pots. These words, such as 'Snore and you sleep alone', made them attractive as humorous gifts to bring home to relatives. Their products are largely sgraffito, which is dealt with in the next chapter.

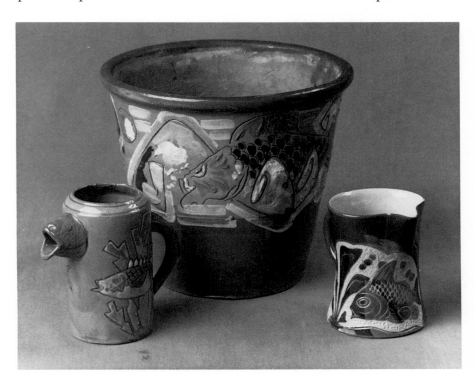

Two fish jugs and a flower pot from Brannams of Barnstaple, showing sgraffito and slip painting in the 'Liberty's' style.

The demise of the rural potteries

Although making mainly souvenirs, the South Devon potteries still continued to produce functional wares, such as hair-tidys, matchbox holders, egg cups and tea pots. It is very easy to scoff at these whimsical pots, but anyone who has struggled to master slipware techniques will realize how skilled was their application of slip, and will feel sad that very specific and unusual skills of slip application have disappeared along with the potteries themselves.

Looking back at the economic factors that caused the collapse of so many pottery businesses, both small and large, during the last one hundred years, one is forced to conclude that even if a flexible attitude to trends and fashions was maintained, it could not prolong the life of a workshop indefinitely. The combination of various factors makes it very easy to understand the present sad situation in which only four authentic country potteries are still in existence in the whole of the United Kingdom. Studying the production of the rural potteries that have survived, one must conclude that it is the integrity of their work which makes their operation valid. Fashions may come and go, but the traditional forms, providing they are well potted and still fulfil their original function, have a permanent place in vernacular art.

South Devon wares from the Aller Vale Pottery. The large vase on the right shows the decoration known as 'scandy'.

6 English sgraffito wares

Sgraffito design under a clear glaze on a large jug attributed to Ralph Shaw, *c.* 1730. *The Wallace Collection.*

In the Bronze Age and earlier, marks were cut into the clay body of pots, but for the purpose of this book our definition of sgraffito ware is to be an image scratched through a coloured slip to reveal the clay body or a contrasting slip below. This technique was well known in Italy in the fifteenth century, which is why the process has kept its Italianate name.

The Beauvais pots from France are of major interest, as these show examples of the strongest and most complex sgraffito wares. It is hard to understand the particular elaboration of the Beauvais technique. The pot was thrown in white clay, slipped in red clay and, as an added refinement, then slipped in a white clay of the same colour as the body. The wording and decoration were beautifully incised with a toothed metal tool, to reveal only the red slip – the skills needed to do this were remarkable. Finally the whole pot is enhanced with brushstrokes of copper, manganese and cobalt under a transparent glaze. Southampton Museum, in England, has an excellent example

of this Beauvais ware – an early sixteenth-century ornate sgraffito mug with an inscription *nul bien sans pene* (no good without pain).

There is often a design of a face in the centre of Beauvais sgraffito plates which leads one to make comparisons with sixteenth-century Italian majolica, but it is noticeable that the French pieces have a strong and noble 'Gothic' character (see page 58) quite different from the realistic presentations on the Italian plates.

There are also stylized floral and geometric motifs found on these French wares. Only one complete pot has been excavated in England, although sherds are fairly evenly distributed in port sites.

This wonderful work, slipped and engraved with fine lines and a toothed instrument, was not to continue: by the seventeenth century it was superseded by the use of the horn trailer. This method of decoration continued, particularly in southern France, until the 1960s when it was largely replaced by painted decoration on a tin glaze.

Beauvaisis plate from the sixteenth century, with the head of a young man in sgraffito, surrounded by the motto 'Better late than never'. 9″ diameter. *Rouen Museum.*

North Devon ware

The situation was not the same in England, for there is no record of elaborate sgraffito wares being made until the seventeenth century, when Bideford in North Devon became prosperous. In the sixteenth century, Queen Elizabeth I had granted a modern charter of incorporation for the town to Sir Richard Grenville. He was one of the first explorers of Virginia with Sir Walter Raleigh, and trade developed with Maryland and Virginia. Fragments of Devon harvest jugs have been excavated in New England, as have sherds of the local clay bread-ovens that continued until the 1930s to be a speciality of the Bideford potters.* After 1600 the tradition of Devon sgraffito wares was fairly continuous, the jugs being made in eight different potteries in Bideford over a period of two centuries. Although Devon pitchers were exported to America in the seventeenth century, there is scant evidence of their being a source of inspiration to the local American potters (many of whom had immigrated from Germany, Switzerland, Slovakia and Holland, bringing with them their own traditions), the most famous being the Pennsylvanian Dutch ('Deutsch') potters, renowned for their decorative 'tulipware'.

*Fishley-Holland, in his book *Forty Years a Potter*, gives a graphic description of the making of these ovens.

The North Devon potteries were situated close to a tidal stream, allowing clay to be brought in and pots to be taken out. There is a theory that these North Devon potteries were influenced by Beauvais wares, as much of it was being imported into this part of the country. However, I can see little relationship between the bold and rustic English pots and the more refined French wares. There was much commerce between Bideford (and nearby Barnstaple) and ports in Holland and Normandy, and there are even some indications that immigrants were working in Bideford at this time. One always looks for pattern and inspirational sources, but inspiration has to start somewhere and I see no reason to suppose that a method of working and decoration did not originate in Devon.

These wares were twice-fired – unusual in the seventeenth century – but a working potter will appreciate that large jugs (often 14 inches high), covered as they were with words and pictures, were particularly vulnerable to damage before firing and would have been difficult to raw glaze. Whilst archaeologists and historians have

A moulded dish, 'Vase of Flowers', from Pennsylvania, dated 1818. The sgraffito design is supplemented with orange slip and copper oxide, pale honey glaze. 11″ diameter.

English sgraffito wares

their own reactions to both the archive and the finds in the Bideford area, a working potter views the output in a much more down-to-earth way. Despite the early kilns' being exposed to the elements, and the inadequate buildings (often scarcely more than lean-to sheds) of the early potteries, some of the circumstances would not have changed, such as marketing and competition. Work had to be priced competitively, new ideas had to be thought up each year, pots had to be delivered promptly if the potters were to survive. Despite all these hazards, the potters who made the harvest jugs of North Devon achieved remarkable standards, both of beauty and execution. They have a particular Englishness, covered as they are with pictures of ships and flowers (particularly the primrose) and poems celebrating the joys of drinking cider. These great jugs form quite an unusual group of pots in the English tradition as they depict and reflect life in Bideford. Most other English slipwares are decorated with formalized designs such as kings and queens, and tulips, with little relation to the seasons and the daily round of a working man's life.

Bideford was a strong Puritan community, hard working and God-fearing, and no doubt this contributed to its wealth. It did not prevent its potters, however, from scratching humorous, not to say bibulous, inscriptions on their pots. The spontaneity of the simple line drawings and the traditional poems on the Bideford wares is very moving. The great cider jugs, celebrating the gathering of the harvest and sheep-shearing, are often very elaborate, many being drawn with ships and inscribed with the recipients' name as well as two or three lines of simple poetry; for example, 'Long may we live, happy may we be, blest with content and from misfortune free; Mary Palmer, 2 January 1861.' At the other end of the scale, some jugs are only five inches high and these are particularly endearing.

In the Bideford tradition, each size of pitcher had a name: yellow drum, red pitcher, long Tom, forty tales, gullymouths, pinchguts, sixties and penny jugs.

Left Devon harvest jug from Bideford, 18″ high. Sgraffito revealing red clay under honey coloured glaze. *Right* animal group by George Fishley, nineteenth century. 6″ high, 9″ wide.

Beere-Fishley jug, 1841. 12″ high.

Henry Phillips, of East-the-Water pottery in Bideford, was still working at the beginning of the twentieth century and his pottery can be seen in the Burton Art Gallery in Bideford. He worked in a disciplined way, enhancing the main designs with soft brushed cobalt under a clear glaze. This was uncommon – copper oxide was generally used under a honey glaze.

The early work of the Fishley family of Fremington pottery, situated between Bideford and Barnstaple, was probably derived from the Donyatt (Somerset) applied decoration, but each generation of the family contributed something new. Earliest of these was George Fishley (1771–1865), perhaps one of the most important single

61

earthenware potters of the nineteenth century. He made watch pockets, animal groups, portrait figures, etc., each of these being modelled in a marvellously uninhibited manner. He was the first of the English coarseware potters to build free-standing figures from his own experience, as opposed to copying the antique. Some potters were doing the latter at the same period but the results were unsatisfactory. One must recognize how unusual it was for a country potter to create original work of value, as, generally speaking, the arduous nature of the trade kept them tied to the wheel and the workshop, fulfilling orders. They had little time for any exploration of the medium.

Pottery was a useful trade, in the nineteenth century, like blacksmithing, tinsmithing, baking and carpentry. Generally the business was passed on from father to son, but this did not always mean that artistic talents were inherited. Luckily, George Fishley's two sons, Edmund (d. 1861) and Robert, also produced excellent examples of applied decoration, especially the Bideford Wassail Cup which can be seen in Exeter Museum. Edmund's son, Edwin Beere Fishley (d. 1911), continued to make traditional harvest jugs and also produced a wide range of wares, constantly adapting new ideas to enable the pottery to survive the economic and aesthetic changes of the nineteenth century.

W. Fishley Holland joined the Fremington pottery in 1902 and became its manager on the death of his grandfather. But the pottery was sold to a Staffordshire firm in 1912, at which time Fishley Holland moved to Braunton and then to Clevedon in Somerset. In the early stages his work was in the Fremington tradition but softer in execution and glossier; the handles of the sheep-shearing jugs continued to have the traditional scroll at the base and he made many of the typical old Fremington pots. When he moved to Braunton and later to Clevedon he experimented with turquoise, blue and even pink glazes to attempt to capture the new 'Art' market. This work was interesting but rarely inspired. Perhaps his greatest contribution was the book that he published in 1958, *'Forty Years a Potter'*, which gives a matchless account of the way a country potter lived and worked in the

Sgraffito decoration on bread-oven door. Bideford.

early part of the twentieth century. This is one inscription he often scratched into his jugs:

'Fill me full of liquor sweet for that is good
　　when friends do meet
When friends do meet and liquor plenty
Fill me again when I.B.M.T.'

The Fremington clay, from which these jugs were made, was quarried locally and supplied not only to Barnstaple but to places as far away as Wales, Cornwall and Ireland, which is not surprising, bearing in mind the wonderful plastic quality of the material. William Fishley Holland writes of his clay:

> It has been used for generations by all North Devon potters, it is chocolate in colour, fires a beautiful terra cotta and matures at 1000 degrees Centigrade which is a great advantage, combined with its strength for throwing and pulling handles. I know of no other clay which can be thrown so thin when one has acquired the necessary experience.

There is a record of $1\frac{1}{2}$ tons of this Fremington clay being sent by sea from Bideford to St Ives in 1684. Pack horse deliveries would not have been recorded. A clayworker's ton contained 70 balls, weighing 35 to 36 lbs each. A pack horse could not carry more than six 9 inch cubes, so a string of twelve horses was needed to transport a ton of clay.

Fine gravel was essential to temper the clay for coarser wares that had to adapt to changes of temperature, such as cooking pots and bread ovens. John Watkins, the Bideford historian, wrote:

> The earthenware made here is generally supposed to be superior to any other of the kind, and this is accounted for from the peculiar excellence of the *gravel* which this river affords, in binding the clay. That this is the true reason seems clear, from the fact that though the potteries at Barnstaple make use of the same sort of clay yet their earthenware is not held in such esteem at Bristol, etc., as that of Bideford.

For glazing, some galena was also probably obtained from local sources, near Yarnscombe and Torrington, but most of the lead was shipped from Wales, in particular from Aberdovey. There is no archaeological evidence to show what fuel was used in the seventeenth century to fire the wares, but from the appearance of the pots and the well-wooded nature of the countryside, it must be assumed that wood was used. Brannams of Barnstaple certainly fired their kilns with this material until the 1880s. Faggots of furze were used to bring the kilns up to temperature. A certain Mr Those of Bideford wrote in 1632:

> We do plainely perceive the great danger and misery which divers of the Inhabitants of this Towne are in especiallie those that lie neere unto such places where the potters' kills [kilns] are, by means that diverse of them do burn their kills with furses and breures [briars] and such flayming fuell and many of them do place and putt their Rickes of furse and Bruers eyther neere unto the said kills or betwixt their dwelling houses and their kills whereby much hurte may suddenly happen to this Towne.

I have myself seen just such a method of firing in Granada, where the furze ricks were the same size as the old fashioned hay rick, and where none of the drying difficulties such as were obvious in Bideford were evident, but I imagine the nuisance value would have been even worse.

In conclusion, it will be seen that these North Devon potters were very well situated, having the best clay, the gravel, the fuel and the transport all readily available. Most important of all, they had the skills and the imagination to exploit all these advantages. Many of the poems inscribed on their wares will be found in chapter 9.

Enid Marx and Margaret Lambert, wrote in their book *English Popular Art* in 1951:

> The innocent eye is disappearing in England, not, we think, entirely due to mechanisation but rather from changing social habits, bringing a certain lack of initiative and interest in things with an individual character. . . . which gave life to the old popular art.

One hopes that since the 1950s and 60s attitudes have changed a little, and now there is more appreciation of vernacular pottery and folk art in general.

Perhaps the most widely known North Devon earthenware was that of C. H. Brannam, who took over the Litchdon Street Pottery, Barnstaple, in 1879, after having served a long apprenticeship in two of his father's earlier potteries. Initially, they made some fairly crude country-style sgraffito jugs and tygs, using the pure red Fremington clay. They then rapidly moved into making art wares, which were sold to Liberty's as early as 1880.

Originally, the design was scratched through the white slip to the red body and covered with a clear or honey glaze, but later their simple forms were covered with brown, blue or green slips and elaborately scratched back to the white. This work is now widely collected.

Charles Brannam died in 1937, and although the premises remain unaltered, during his son Peter's tenure the art wares ceased. Traditional wares, such as pitchers, planters and bread-crocks, continue to be made successfully under the present owner, and a wide range of jigger-and-jolleyed flower-pots is also produced.

Ewenny, South Wales

Ewenny is south of the market town of Bridgend in the Vale of Glamorgan. There is excellent boulder clay to be found in deep deposits, and galena for the glaze could be dug nearby. There is some archival evidence that pottery has been made in this area since medieval times, but it was in the early part of the eighteenth century that fifteen potteries were working here, mainly producing useful vessels for farm dairies and kitchens: milk pans, bowls, churns, wash-bowls, porringers and chamber pots. There were also a few slip-trailed decorated wares for presentation pieces, like money boxes and puzzle jugs, as well as the famous Wassail bowls.

At New Year, parties of 'wassailers' would call at all the local houses, greeting the inmates

A wassail cup from Ewenny, with sgraffito decoration and the following inscription on the lid: 'Gift to Mr William Cox, House of Correction Swansea, from Mr Morgan Morgans Road Surveyor Bridgend September 23d 1836. Made at Claypits'.

and drinking a concoction of spiced ale, sometimes with the addition of apples. The locals would dress up in elaborate costume and the wassail bowl itself would echo this fancy-dress with its multiple handles, and the figure of a man astride the barrel. By the 1880s, the custom appears to have died out and the surviving bowls date from 1825 to 1845.

The decline in the industry was halted in the 1880s by a reawakened interest in decorated art wares, some of which were ornamented with resist leaf decoration – a hideous technique which was also used occasionally in North Devon. Soft natural leaves with their stems were pressed on to the moist thrown pots and the whole was dipped in slip. When leather-hard, the leaf was pulled away, or it could be left to burn off in the kiln. This method of decoration has survived like a persistant weed in school pottery classes and Further Education classes into the 1980s as a simple but tasteless method of decoration.

Ewenny as a pottery centre suffered a decline in production at the turn of the century. It is too easy to blame both the competition from Staffordshire transfer printed wares and the general increased transport facilities: the rigidity and the lack of enterprise of these country potteries contributed to their own demise. When the sons of family-owned potteries received further education at art schools, and even visited the Metropolis, they injected new blood and contributed fresh ideas. As a result of this, some potteries in Ewenny survived just into the twentieth century producing fanciful or flexible designs, particularly for sale by Liberty's.

Donyatt, Somerset

The other well-known district specializing in sgraffito ware was Donyatt, in the Vale of Taunton Deane in Somerset. This was a thriving pottery centre in medieval times but its flowering was in the seventeenth century. Puzzle jugs, fuddling cups (jolly-boys), multiple flower vases and commemorative plates were made and decorated in the sgraffito technique.

Fuddling cups have been made since medieval

Tulipière from Donyatt in Somerset, seventeenth century, sgraffito with splashes of copper.

retained the white slip background, the drawing being linear and employing largely geometric motifs. The generous lead glaze was splattered with copper green. One of the most famous large Donyatt plates is dated 1680 and depicts the birth of a pair of female Siamese twins, Aquilla and Priscilla. Apparently they were abducted by a certain Captain Watrond and Sir Edward Phillips, who kept and exhibited them for money until their death. Recording the same phenomenon, which must have been remarkable in its time, two Lambeth tin-glazed plates were also made showing the abductors in Charles II costume, supporting the Siamese twins and with the inscription: 'Behold to Parsons that are reconsid to rob the parents and to keep the child.' One of these plates can be seen in Truro Museum.

Buckley, North Wales

Buckley in Clwyd, near Chester, had coal for firing the kilns, a good red pot-clay, a fine white clay, coarser brick clays, and also an excellent variety of fireclay and stoneware clays.

The earliest find of pots from this district dates to the thirteenth century. Many of these were baluster-shaped, lead-glazed jugs. The potteries were busy from the fourteenth to the seventeenth century, making domestic wares such as dairy pots, pancheons and ridge tiles. By the seventeenth and eighteenth centuries, the range of wares made had expanded considerably, and included beakers, cups, tygs, tankards, coal pots, jugs, possets and chamber pots. Clay pipes were also made, exploiting the use of the good white clay available.

A large number of the wares were decorated with slip, either scratched or trailed. Many of these pots were transported on the River Dee to Chester but it was not until 1737, when a new channel was cut, avoiding the silted areas of the river, that trade could thrive. This included the bricks and firebricks that were now being made, the latter for furnace linings, wash house slop stones, pig troughs and grave headstones.

John Catherall, who started the fireclay business in the eighteenth century, also built a brickworks, and his potteries were producing

times, to confuse drinkers who would try to drink from one of the little cups, only to find the liquor flowing into another. There were often from three to six of these containers, joined by looped and twisted hollow handles.

It would appear that Donyatt specialized in making these joined pots. There are several complete ones extant, decorated through the white slip with wide and bold sgraffito designs and the Donyatt trade mark, great splashes of copper green.

Slip-trailed wares were also made here in the seventeenth century – dishes with banding and some combing, white on the red body, as well as cups and chamber pots. Large functional pans and containers with handsome finger-impressed decoration (as an unglazed coil) continued to be made at Donyatt into the late nineteenth century.

It is worth noting that in 1910 Dr Glaisher of Cambridge, the famous ceramic collector, commissioned an ornate money box to be made here and inscribed with his name. This must have been one of the last pots produced in Donyatt, as the pottery finally closed after the First World War.

The main difference between this work and the Devon wares was that in Somerset they

coaster

tobacco jar

John Hay
1870

Ship trailed plate

Buckley ware.

basins, plates, bread-pans, ham salters, flower pots and butter dishes which were exported to Ireland as well as used in Wales. The Staffordshire factory-made white wares did not really affect this market, as the users needed cheap everyday objects. Nevertheless, in the 1830s and 1840s the quality of the wares was subject to criticism, and gradually by the end of the nineteenth century there was a diminishing number of pottery works.

Art wares of a rustic nature, as well as novelty wares, were produced, the best of which were the tiered money boxes ornamented with birds, both slip-trailed and scratched, and the small ornamental chests of drawers and cuckoo whistles. One of the other unusual lines were the table coasters, very useful when woodworm shortened table legs which were being continually soaked as the floor was scrubbed. Several country potteries, including Burton in Lonsdale, made these, as well as moulded piano coasters for protecting carpets.

Jim Bentley, the chemist of Buckley who has made a life long study of the potteries, recounts that George Lamb, an old man now, whose father was one of the last potters, told him that they would use no other than Halkyn lead (galena) as a glaze and no other coal than from the Point of Ayr colliery. They also made certain secret local additions. Jim Bentley also says that in the nineteenth century delicate Buckley earthenware, which would be readily damaged by repeated handling, was often transferred to Connah's Quay docks by special boxes. These 'shipping boxes' had an iron post at each corner with a large ring at the top, and were loaded and taken along tram rails to the local exchange siding. Between two and eight of them were run at a time on to a railway wagon, with narrow-gauge transverse lines across its floor. The train load of these loaded boxes was taken to the docks alongside the boat. If they were to be taken to Liverpool for re-shipment, the individual boxes were lifted by the rings and placed in the hold of a lighter. The loaded lighter then sailed across to Liverpool and the export warehouses, the cargo not having been

Right **charger by Thomas Toft 'King Charles in the oak', 20″ diameter. Note the miniscule pearling on the outlines of the drawing, and remember this was done with a pouring vessel.**

Top left a loving cup 11″ wide from Staffordshire, slip trailed with pearling. One of the few seventeenth-century Staffordshire pots with a clear, as opposed to honey coloured, glaze. *Left* bowl, Wanfried-an-der-Werra, sixteenth century, 30″ diameter, with white slip trailing and sgraffito. *Above* Thomas Toft charger, 'The Temptation'. 22″ diameter, seventeenth century. Slip-trailed on black engobe under a clear glaze. The unusual grey-green slip is similar to that on the egg stand and winged cup shown on page 34.

An impress-moulded dish, 14½″ diameter, early eighteenth century, one of a series made by Samuel Malkin. This particular one, showing two figures, is inscribed 'wee three logerheads', implying that the spectator provides the third. It may be derived from an inn sign in the village of Loggerheads, twenty-five miles from Burslem, Staffordshire.

English sgraffito wares

touched en route — an early example of the container concept over a short distance.

Jim Bentley discovered some remarkable seventeenth-century wasters which have been identified as sgraffito platters, probably drawn from a Bestiary, originally produced in the fifteenth century (see *Seventeenth-century bestiary ware from Buckley, Clwyd*, K. Lloyd Gruffydd). These platters, when the fragments were put together, show elements of strange birds and elephants and fragmented inscriptions round the rim which point to their origin. Much of this legendary material is tied in with Christian iconography, and is always of interest as one seeks to discover design sources on pottery. There are two strange bird dishes in the Sheffield City Museum and one in Stoke which may also be derived from the Bestiary.

I have never thought it of value to look into a much deeper psychological and philosphic significance in folk pottery patterns — the job of the potter is to please his clients and to make enough money to support his dependents. If in the process he enjoys his work, it will sell better.

The flowering of the Buckley potteries was in the seventeenth century and latterly in the nineteenth century, with their handsome flower-pot shaped milk pots, white inside and black out, or sometimes just black slip over the red body which was dark and often made murky with the sulphurous fumes from the coal firing. All this work was once-fired, like seventeenth-century Staffordshire wares.

The closure of the last of the Buckley potteries by World War II marked the end of six-hundred years of pot making.

South Devon

The South Devon potteries in the Torquay district (Watcombe, Royal Torquay and particularly Aller Vale) in the 1880s produced some sgraffito ware inspired by the antique pots, but later developed their own specific 'souvenir' wares. This enabled them to withstand the economic pressures that forced other potteries to close. Jolly sayings were

Buckley ware.

H 20cm

= milk pot not bread bin

fragment
of bestiary
dish

A group of South Devon wares from the Aller Vale Pottery, showing slip trailing, painting and sgraffito.

scratched boldly into the white slip on pots that ranged from tea pot and cream jug to hair tidy and hair-curler rest. They were designed for and bought by day-trippers from the industrial regions of Britain, and therefore became spread over a wide area.

> O list to me ye Ladies fair
> And when you wish to
> Curl your hair
>
> For the safety
> of this
> domicile
> Place
> Your lamps upon this tile

These South Devon potteries developed a highly skilled technique of painting on the slips in an almost *pâte-sur-pâte* technique, brushing and trailing brightly coloured slips on to the red body, and then applying a transparent glaze.

Everyone knows South Devon wares but few people recognize them as elaborate slipware, and unfortunately the particular method of applying the slip skilfully in bold relief is now lost. Although these pots are collected by a few enthusiasts, I feel the time has come to recognize the unusual technical skill employed in their

making, and to place them in their interesting sociological setting.

The industry began because of the chance find of a bed of fine red clay in the grounds of Watcombe House near Torquay in 1869. Queen Victoria graciously accepted a pair of Watcombe water bottles in 1873, and this of course guaranteed the success of the pottery. More clay was discovered and other potteries opened: the Torquay Terra Cotta Company, Hele Cross, the Torquay Pottery, Longpark and various other smaller establishments. Aller Vale, the most interesting of all, was situated between Kingskerswell and Newton Abbot. Originally this pottery made ordinary domestic wares, then later architectural pottery such as roofing tiles, drainage pipes, garden edgings, ornamental chimney pots and some flower vases.

In 1879 an art school was founded by Mr Phillips, the owner of the Aller Vale pottery, in a cottage nearby. This enterprise flourished and Mr Phillips gave lectures on the Arts and Crafts Movement. He was a well known local historian and antiquarian, and it was he who encouraged George Fishley of Fremington to copy antique pots in the British Museum. Although originally Mr Phillips' idea was philanthropic, he did employ some of the art students in his pottery. Japanese, Egyptian, Persian and Italian styles were the inspiration for the Aller Vale forms, as well as some old English shapes. The work was advertized as 'Faience', which means painting on to the white tin-oxide glaze before firing, but Devonshire Faience of the Aller Vale pottery was wheel-thrown in the red clay and dipped in white slip, and then decorated underglaze with designs in coloured slips. The relief quality of these slips is unusual, as is the intensity of colour, particularly the dark olive-green which comes from chrome.

Unfortunately, most of the excellent books written about these potteries are not by working potters and the authors fail to explain the techniques. I find some of the methods of building up the slips extraordinary, for they cling so tightly to the surface slip and body, showing no signs of peeling although thickly applied. The glaze is excellent and hard-wearing, and after one hundred years they show

no signs of crazing: 'a match for any man', as was inscribed on a match-holder and striker.

Part of the Four Seasons plate by Edward Bingham, Castle Hedingham, nineteenth century. Applied decoration, polychrome. 16" diameter. *Colchester Museum.*

Essex

Brannams of Barnstaple produced work from the 1890s to the 1930s that was inspired partly by the antique but always geared to a market, whereas Edward Bingham of the Castle Hedingham pottery in Essex was an eccentric, an artist, with little business aptitude. Often the work is not intrinsically beautiful, but his skill in modelling and firing this unpromising red clay with only the use of lead glaze was remarkable. The influence of Palissy, Beauvais and Wrotham pottery, as well as the classic forms, is clear to see.

The story of Bingham's life and times is remarkable. His family moved to Castle Hedingham, Essex, in 1837 when he was eight years old. His father set up a pottery making simple functional pots for the villagers out of the coarse local red clay. Edward himself was always interested and showed considerable skill in modelling at an early age, but his father apprenticed him to a bootmaker. He later went to work as a school assistant where he became interested in the antique. Returning to the pottery on his father's death, he made many copies of seventeenth-century puzzle jugs, tygs, etc., including a famous replica of the Porsenna Vase. During the 1880s, Edward Bingham worked as a sub-postmaster and was helped by his son, yet another Edward, in the pottery, where there were as many as 13 kilns in operation.

In 1889, young Edward took over and sold the pottery (when it was renamed the Essex Art Pottery) though he continued to act as manager. In 1905 it closed. Edward emigrated to America where a year later his father, now aged 76, joined him.

I think it is possible that some of the slipwares made by Bingham as copies of the antique, for example Wrotham or Metropolitan tygs, may still confuse the experts and I have wondered if some of the larger possets at one time attributed to Fareham, were not from his hand. This work was never intended to deceive, but was the outcome of Bingham's fascination with the past and his attempts to master the elusive slipware skills. Colchester Museum holds a considerable body of his work.

73

Michael Cardew.
Slip trailed bird
dish with white
slip and copper
decoration.
$16\frac{3}{4}''$ wide.

7

Twentieth-century studio slipware in England

When the studio pottery movement was started in the early part of the twentieth century, the first pots made by Bernard Leach and his followers were in the Japanese style, but there was a period when he and Michael Cardew discovered the work of the English seventeenth-century potters and some vivid slipwares were produced at St Ives. Bernard Leach, in *A Potter's Book*, says: 'We saw that there were definite limitations to the use of slipware in present-day

life. The softness and relative roughness of the ware relegates it for the most part to the kitchen and the cottage . . . But few people want red and brown or black or heavy cream-coloured ware for table use in modern cities.'

The technical difficulties faced by Leach were formidable. It takes about ten years to develop trailing skills and to get the slip, the clay and the glaze to match satisfactorily. If your heart is not in it you may well give up, and making inspired 'copies' of seventeenth-century chargers with buckled rims and pitted surfaces did not create a satisfactory product for the studio market, as did the excellent range of tenmoku glazed domestic stoneware that was subsequently produced at St Ives. However, Michael Cardew, after his move from Cornwall to Winchcombe in Gloucestershire, continued to make some lovely slipware pieces.

Subsequently, many potters were introduced by the influential Dora Billington of the Central School of Art, London, to the mysteries of slip-trailing, including Ron Cooper, Paul Barron, Henry Hammond, Mick Casson, John Solly, William Newland and others. I illustrate on the following pages some of the work from the 1940s to the 1960s that interests me.

There is a small group of earthenware potters working with slips nowadays whose work I admire and this group is expanding. More and more potters are excited by the medium but daunted by the process.

The precursor of modern slipware potters, the maverick among the students of Staite-Murray at the Royal College of Art, was Sam Haile, one of the few potters to have used the slip-trail medium in a dynamic way. Uneasy with the more formal approach of other students, he experimented with freer forms and methods of

Bird's head bowl by Jason Shackleton, sgraffito. 15″ diameter.

'Friends' by Alan Frewin. Plate, 15″ diameter, with white, black, dark brown, tan and blue slip, pearled, trailed and painted under honey glaze.

decoration. After a period as teacher at Leicester College of Art, he married the potter Marianne de Trey, and they left for the USA. After a shaky start doing menial jobs his work was seen in New York and this led to teaching at New York College of Ceramics, where his work had a profound effect on the previously perfectionist methods of his peers and on the whole American ceramic movement. In 1947, Sam Haile and Marianne de Trey returned to England where he began making slipware again. What was particularly interesting and unusual about his work was the complete rejection of traditional slipware decoration and the spontaneous application of decorative motifs, mainly abstract in form, trailed on to large 'modernistic' vases and dishes. These abstract designs were made at the same time as a group of figuratively decorated pots. Simplified nudes dance and recline against the rough clay surface. Perhaps the most notorious of these pots is the Cerne Abbas giant, 36 inches high, a monumental piece made in stoneware. This was unique, as it showed for the first time some relationship to contemporary painting.

It was not until 1945 at Bulmer in Suffolk, that Haile later began to work in earthenware, using local brick clays but with less sand; this clay fired to a pleasant greenish-yellow. He used principally a manganese black slip, a white one less often. Much of the decoration was combed or finger-patterned and many jugs were slipped sideways or poured, resulting curved shapes on the pot being used skilfully and simply as part of the overall design. The pots were coal-fired to about 1060–1080°C and the glaze was either red-lead or galena. Sometimes this glaze or the coal-firing (after the Second World War coal in Britain was of low quality) caused 'scumming' on the pot. Despite this, the best of the pots had a lovely colour and texture, quite unlike that obtained with a fritted lead glaze. The smaller pots were placed in saggars, but the large ones were exposed to the flames, sitting on top of the saggars.

Some of the work during the Bulmer period was trailed in white on a black background with very little infilling. In Marianne de Trey's collection is a beautiful dish, 13 inches in diameter, called 'Piccaninny and Mère', on which all the white drawing lines are enhanced by black pearling. Many of his plates have both a male and female figure on them. There is a wholeness about Sam Haile's pots because form and design blend completely. It would be correct to say that his style anticipated the ceramic work of Picasso.

Haile was tragically killed in 1948, and the flow of this work was stopped. It is time for a re-appraisal of his pottery, some of which can be seen in the Victoria & Albert Museum, London.

Beach scene 1937 by Sam Haile. 12″ diameter, slip trailed and painted.

Annunciation dish, Wanfried-an-der-Werra, dated 1590. Sgraffito, white engobe on red body, painted copper, cut-out background, white slip trail banded and with rim decoration.

8 Continental slipwares

It is the purpose of this chapter to record and describe as many as possible of the remarkable slip wares to be found in Europe, from the elaborate sgraffito techniques of Beauvais in France in the early seventeenth century to the complexities of German dishes made in the eighteenth century, and beyond.

A marvellous range of varied slipware has been made in an unbroken tradition right across Europe. Naturally the export endeavours of some countries in the past have made their wares more familiar than others, but with widespread travel the domestic pottery which has been made for centuries in many lands is now widely exposed to view. Unfortunately, catering for a tourist industry has a dulling and debasing effect on pottery, whether slipware or majolica, but local museums in small towns in countries as far apart as France and Poland usually have collections showing the vernacular ware of the past, and these are inspiring to modern potters, just as they are instructive to collectors.

Germany

There is no doubt that the slip wares produced in Germany from the sixteenth century to the present day are the most interesting in the whole of the continent. In the first place the size of many of the wheel-thrown dishes is remarkable, some of those made in the seventeenth and eighteenth centuries being three feet in diameter. The pale orange clay body is very light and these great chargers can be easily lifted in the hand.

The Niederrhein area alone has about forty villages, each containing many potteries producing elaborately decorated ware, using all the techniques available to the lead-glazed earthenware potter, many of them being applied on a single dish. As well as scratching, trailing, painting and cutting, bold pads of clay were often applied on the large wall-plates. Much of the work has a religious theme as this is predominantly a Roman Catholic area. Tiles were also made in this area, many of which were

for the traditional stoves, but some also for fireplaces (see facing page).

Duisburg, Glimbach, Hüls, Issum, Rayen, Schaephuysen, Sevelen, also made amusing and decorative tiles, principally in the sgraffito technique. Some of these were used for wall decoration, like pictures. Also typical of the Niederrhein were the spoon racks, holy water stoups, couvre-feux, Dutch ovens and Gügelhopf (cake) moulds.

The Fitzwilliam Museum in Cambridge and the Victoria & Albert Museum in London contain many of these pots, and there is a great deal of published material on this slipware available in Germany (see bibliography). In this chapter I describe only a small sample of German work, treating the centres, for convenience of sequence, in alphabetical order.

Frechen Many of the dishes made in this area have black rims and slip-trailed white centres, and the subjects represented are frequently, religious. There is a graphic depiction of the Flight into Egypt, also a stark Crucifixion. Madonna and Child are lovingly drawn and all the Frechen work is excellently done, using the sgraffito technique. Some of the work is pure fun – such as two gentlemen sitting either side of the table on chairs, sharing one platter and a bottle of wine. One, with a row of cocky young soldiers marching straight across the plate with shouldered arms, is done with lively brush strokes in a very impressionist manner. This pottery has a long history, but the particular work which charms me comes from the eighteenth century.

In **Helenabrunn** the dishes have narrower rims and are slip-trailed in a delicate way, but with not such good drawing – the drawing is rather similar to those on the rustic English Devon harvest jugs. One unusual subject scratched on these dishes is a windmill and tulip, quite unlike all the other subjects from the Niederrhein.

In **Hoerstgen** there is a pronounced vine or grape decoration on the inner rim of many of the

Left **Adam and Eve fireplace from the second half of the eighteenth century, Niederrhein. Painting, trailing and sgraffito in green and brown under honey glaze. On the wall are some fine slipware dishes.**

dishes, and also the recurring tulip and star design. Two of these wonderful dishes can be seen in the Fitzwilliam Museum in Cambridge, measuring 25 inches and 20 inches in diameter. Most of the Hoerstgen wares are sgraffito-decorated rather than slip trailed, with the background slip cut away to reveal the red body clay, and the main forms enhanced with brushed copper oxide.

Hüls was a very prolific pottery area where about thirty named potters worked in the eighteenth century. Many pots are dated 1730. The drawing on all the work is crisp and excellent, the subject being principally religious and often very moving, particularly the Pietà, with its weeping mother and a bitter scene of the Crucifixion. A rich reddish-black slip is used on a white background. I can imagine these great dishes looking splendid on the walls of municipal buildings and in the rich burghers' houses.

Issum. Some of the ware from Issum is earlier than that of Hüls and is often almost three-dimensional, with a great deal of applied decoration in relief which is then slipped under a clear glaze. Sgraffito work was also made here, often with the whole background cut away around the drawing, to reveal the body and produce a contrasting effect. There is a magnificent plate attributed to Issum in the Glaisher Collection, Fitzwilliam Museum, Cambridge (see illustration on back cover of this book).

In **Rayen** the pots have a white background with an elaborate geometric rim decoration, and the vine design is also used. There are inscriptions under the illustrations, which are often of farming and rural subjects. Towards the end of the eighteenth century, several dishes with religious themes were produced. One unusual plate has a feathered rim and cut out background – feathering is a technique rarely seen in mainland Europe. Adam and Eve were also favourite subjects, the drawing having the same sort of naïveté as seen on the English tin-glaze seventeenth-century chargers.

Rheurdt, also in the Niederrhein, produced

Horse and rider dish, sgraffito, inscribed 'Peter Menten Anno 1739', from Rheurdt. White engobe, multi-coloured painting.

rather less skillfully made and decorated dishes with small rims, densely filled with a wreath design, and bunches of grapes scratched on the inner rim. Most of the pots date between 1735 and 1766. The subjects include weddings, and the horse and rider which occurs so often on these German dishes. The sgraffito technique is employed under a clear glaze, often with the background cut away to reveal the body.

Schaephuysen is a very famous pottery centre, much of the work having a black background, slip trailed with white. There is a vivid series of plates depicting the Stations of the Cross, and a dish which appeals to me shows a wonderful fat horse filling the centre of a 12 inch dish. Much of the work dates from the latter part of the eighteenth century.

In **Raum Schaephuysen** a series of smaller plates, about 12 inches in diameter, was decorated in the sgraffito manner with turreted buildings going across the plate. It is interesting to see a square design on a round dish, and in this instance it is very satisfying.

Sonsbeck. There are dishes from Sonsbeck

dated between 1715 and the 1750s, decorated in relief on a black background. Again the grape is in evidence. Some of the work has a white background and religious subjects are common: the Garden of Eden, Abraham and Isaac, the Expulsion from Paradise and the Journey into Egypt. There is an amusing perspective of the interior of a church during a service with the pastor sermonizing in the pulpit, the congregation in pews, and the choir, all carried out in relief coloured with slips under a clear glaze. Lively sgraffito work on dishes showing village scenes is characteristic of Sonsbeck.

The work from **Vluyn-Vluynsbusch** is amusing and vigorous. Many of the large dishes show men and women dancing and drinking and the plates from here are rather secular. The technique employed is sgraffito on a white ground and dates again from the mid eighteenth century.

The work from **Wickrath** is sophisticated and beautifully drawn, principally on a black background. The prancing horses and riders so common on German dishes are in evidence here, but spectacularly well delineated. There are also a number of plates showing religious themes.

Castle dish from Schaephuysen, 1769. Sgraffito, trailing and multi-coloured decoration, bright yellow glaze.

Modern German ware

There are certain aspects of slipware technique that become clear when one observes master potters in Germany at work now in the twentieth-century tradition. There is a market for elaborately slip-decorated earthenware in Germany, although it sometimes struggles for survival alongside the grey and blue Westerwald salt-glazed wares. These latter pots will be found in local markets, in flea markets, and in all the department stores; their forms are principally derived from the sixteenth to nineteenth century.

Grenzhausen, the focus of pottery in the Westerwald, has three or four slipware potteries and their work is on display alongside the salt-glazed pots.

It is good to visit the wonderful workshop and museum in Grenzhausen of master potter Herr Peltner and his wife, who make a very big range of slip decorated wares: jugs of all sizes, cups, covered candle holders, cockerel candle sticks, small covered cheese dishes, Gugelhopf cake moulds, and figurative wall plaques made from antique spice-biscuit moulds about 12 inches high. The German regulations regarding the presence of lead in the glaze are very stringent, and as the non-lead earthenware glazes are seldom satisfactory, this particular potter has developed a white body and slips that fire to about 1100°C. This he calls 'fine stoneware' and asserts that it will withstand washing-up machines perfectly satisfactorily. He supplies hotels and restaurants, which is a pretty good test for any pottery. It is a successful family pottery business and Herr Peltner has developed an excellent museum of early German pots, both slip and salt glaze, which is housed in part of the display area and in the handsome old bottle-oven. This personal collection has excellent examples of Wanfried-an-der-Werra ware dated 1610, and a great dish of the lower Rhine with applied decoration of the early eighteenth century.

The techniques of decoration practised in Grenzhausen are totally at variance with my own methods. The pots are trailed when they are very dry so that one may handle the slipped pots with no possibility of damaging them. The work is always held in the hand, which is either inside or under the pot, and slip trailed either with a rubber bulb and glass pipette or a small pottery trailer with a fine quill.

In the Peltner pottery there is work on a blue or chrome engobe and a lot of 'sponging', but this is done in quite a different way from what is normally understood by this term. The 'tool' used was foam rubber, applied as either a small round pad about $\frac{1}{8}$ inch thick, or a ring (like a washer), glued on to the base of a chinese brush or stick. These sponges came in many sizes and one was kept for each colour. The slip would be squeezed in small quantities on to a palette and the sponge was dabbed several times on the pot to make the petals of a flower or to form coin-like rings all over a jug. The decorative work is enhanced with a trailer, perhaps to put in a central dot or to make swirls and leaf-like shapes connecting the flowers.

As the work is carried out when the pot is dry, it is possible to draw lightly with a pencil on to slipped bowls. Frau Peltner is a designer by training, and her work is carefully planned beforehand on paper, often with a great deal of excellent lettering. Many wedding plates, rather

Frau Peltner at work.

deeper in shape than the English ones, are made and are specifically wall plates. Slips for these plates are coloured with commercial stains in pretty pinks, blues and yellows under a clear glaze. There is *never* any iron added to the glaze and green is obtained by bright chrome slip.

About half the production in this pottery is jigger and jolleyed and the other half thrown on the wheel. There is only one thrower and the division of labour here is very clear. The owner administrates and does all the technical work, glazes, kilns, etc. His wife is the designer and master decorator, and there are about five apprentices who do the slipping, simple decoration on production ware, jiggering and jolleying, and all the many workshop chores. They are also expected to guide tours of the pottery and its museum, giving the history of salt-glaze wares and a description of the particular type of trailed decoration that is practised by Frau Peltner.

It is interesting also to record the history of one pottery in **Urberach** in Hessen, the Rodgau pottery, which dates back to the fourteenth century and flowered in the seventeenth and eighteenth centuries as a centre of slip-trailed decoration. This continued into the nineteenth century, when Valentin Braun took over his grandfather's pottery. The clay was dug by the family from a rented field. A momentum wheel, common in Europe, was used for throwing the pots, and the pouring slip or engobe was made from a red clay imported from Menigen in Bavaria. Three different coloured slips were used – green, blue and grey – using chrome, cobalt and a blend of these two oxides respectively to form the grey.

Two glaze recipes are recorded:

50 lbs lead	4 lbs lead
20 lbs sand	$1\frac{1}{2}$ lbs sand
5 lb clay	$\frac{1}{2}$ lb clay

The sand would have been pounded and sieved. It is a silica replacement for flint, which is not found in the Urberach.

The decoration on the pots was usually done by the women, and all the sons worked in the pottery although it was known that only the eldest son would inherit.

The kiln was 10 feet long, 5 feet across and over 4 feet high. It held up to 2700 pots of the size of a one-litre (2 pint) milk jug. Until 1931, wood was the fuel used, but from then until 1947 it was fired with coal briquettes, then electricity, and finally, in 1949, oil. This kiln was fired fifty times a year.

Towards the end of the nineteenth century there were marketing problems caused by the production of factory-made enamel and porcelain, a major threat to all rural potters. To compete with this, the Brauns had to increase their production, making pots of a lower quality in their struggle for economic survival, but a young potter who had been sent to art school brought decorating skills and new talents to the pottery, increasing trade and improving its status.

In the early twentieth century, the pottery was divided into two parts, one part producing cheaper functional pottery and the other part producing 'art wares'.

Valentin Braun himself studied in museums and art school and made for his own pleasure many decorative pots in his old age, including art nouveau and Art Deco pieces. Painting with a brush was unknown in Hessen, but Braun used it in the 1930s for decorating coffee sets. These were also 'mass produced', with each worker handling one brush – one blue, one red and the other green. Sponging was used after 1900 but not earlier, and occasionally the whole surface of a pot would be sponged with green and white slip, giving an effect not unlike moss. Sgraffito was used for figurative work and for art nouveau roses. This style of decoration, occurring in England as developed by Macintosh, was widespread throughout Germany in the Edwardian period under the name Jugendstil. Darmstadt Museum contains a massive collection of this work in all disciplines other than ceramics – wood, silver, textiles, and in particular glass. Valentin Braun had some success in the great Hessen competitions and won many prizes. He was signing his work V.B.U.

By 1920 the pottery was mechanized with pug

mills, clay mixers and presses, mechanical wheels and jigger and jolleying machines. It was the biggest pottery in Hessen at this period, and was economically successful whilst also producing experimental work. Pupils came from art school to practise making different types of pots, and new styles of decoration emerged, in particular the jardiniere or 'bodenvase'.

The appearance of plant-pot containers denotes increased wealth in the community. At the present time we so easily accept the garden centre with its massive content of plants and containers, perhaps not realizing the affluence this reflects. For most working people before the nineteenth century, anything so frivolous as tending a potted plant would have been unthinkable.

The artefacts which accompanied peasant life were strictly utilitarian, though fortunately in their decoration we learn something about the pleasures of life. It is always useful to reflect on the habits of earlier country folk, for there is little written information about the people who bought the local potters' wares, and any insight we can gain into their life style will give some indication of what they needed from their local pottery shop.

The forms made at Urberach are interesting and are pleasant enough to survive the passage of time – coffee pot and casserole, wall plate, water, milk, wine and beer jugs. In 1910, coffee *sets* were produced, decorated with intricate slip trailing on to a blue or black and brown background. At the same period another type of coffee set was made but with much simpler decoration, principally circles or 'flowers' formed with dots, requiring little trailing skills. Sometimes these larger circles were sponged and had a few lines incized into them, but on the whole the decoration was rather primitive. By the 1930s, the slip trailer was largely superseded by the brush or sponge applied to the body clay.

After the war, in 1947, fine porcelain was not available so there was a very short boom in rustic pottery, but by the beginning of 1950 this decreased and so the Braun's Rodgau pottery changed to flower-pot production.

At a later date they made extremely rough potted jugs and bowls brushed with the inscription in English, '1958 Greetings from Urberach Germany'. It seems unlikely that an English rural pottery would produce its counterpart, 'Grüsse aus Compton England'.

On the whole, the forms from the Rodgau pottery made by various members of the Braun family were not innovative and the decoration was minimal and traditional. In a sense, the Deco-period is most interesting to an outsider. In England there was no corresponding style developed in rural potteries, where the manufactured pieces from Staffordshire and other factories swamped the market.

Germany is a very large country by comparison to England, and one can perceive that stylistic influences travelled in a much more sophisticated way than they did in England. Also significant is the fact that the public bought and *still* appreciates and buys the pots decorated with the trailer. Visiting the potter in his workplace and seeing him at work is important to the German people, who on the whole have a more serious and respectful approach to the craftsman than their English counterparts.

Holland

Within the last ten years, evidence has been found for much trailed and sgraffito slipware from northern Holland, including dated examples between 1573 and 1711. Many of these forms were exported to England, particularly porringers with two strap side-handles, many with a cockerel design in the centre, white slip on the red sandy body, and sometimes with splashes of copper green.

There are also some larger dishes with dash-type borders and geometric or rosette central decoration, and a splendid Adam and Eve dish picked out in sgraffito. These are dated from 1591 to 1599. There is a natural inclination to assume that seventeenth-century English slipwares were influenced by such decoration, but there seems little similarity between the lively Dutch forms and the somewhat uninspired decoration of, say, the Wrotham wares, or the words and 'firtree' patterns on Metropolitan pots, nor do similar forms or motifs appear on the Staffordshire pottery of the seventeenth and eighteenth century.

The early Dutch shapes and decoration are very similar to the German ones, but this ware in Holland was fairly rapidly superseded by tin-glazed pots from Delft. Much of this was imported to England, and three main centres (Southwark, Bristol and Liverpool) produced 'English Delft' until the eighteenth century. The designs of the famous Staffordshire decorative slip-trailed wares were very similar to some of the early 'naïf' blue and white wares, such as the chargers depicting kings and queens, and the Adam and Eve plates.

It is important not to under-estimate the profound effect on the whole pottery industry across Europe of the massive trade in blue and white pots – Delft – in Britain the impact was from their arrival in East Anglia in the early part of the seventeenth century until the end of the eighteenth century. By this period, Chinese blue and white porcelain was arriving, and this in its turn superseded the tin-glazed wares – because of both its exotic 'rarity' and its hard-wearing qualities.

Switzerland

The Swiss, especially in the Canton of Berne, produced elaborate dishes but in a delicate manner with widespread use of the 'wasp' technique. This was a kind of juddering dot made with a sharpened bent quill, held over the pot in its leather stage as it revolved on the wheel so that the feather hopped, not only leaving the dash marks -------, but making a fine buzzing noise like a wasp. In Hungary this was called the dongo. The forms of the Swiss dishes are sometimes deeper than their German equivalents, and many have a kind of large colander sitting in the top of the dish, designed to hold a potato cake. Most such dishes were highly decorated.

Quill with bent tip for the dongo, wasp or judder technique.

Winterthur was the greatest pottery centre in Switzerland during the seventeenth century, and there are two milk bowls dated 1687 and 1695 in the Basel Volkskunde Museum. Winterthur also supplied large amounts of brightly coloured stove tiles to all the German-speaking Cantons, as well as making every-day decorated household wares.

Langnau in the Emmenthal was also an important area from the seventeenth to the nineteenth century. The wares are principally in a reddish buff body, decorated in a mixture of media : trailing, painting and scratching under a transparent glaze, seldom with the addition of iron. Most of the dishes from Langnau are covered in a white slip, and the scratching and oxide painting is more delicate than that of other districts. Some of the wares are in a bright butter-yellow. This suggests an addition of perhaps $1\frac{1}{2}$ per cent of iron in the glaze. The manganese and copper painting has a tendency to bleed, but this only enhances the decoration. After 1740 blue was used, but only sparingly and under a transparent rather than honey coloured glaze.

Around 1750, as well as the floral and geometric designs, there are many charming

Coffee pot and lid showing the inscription 'Thoune' on the base.

Continental slipwares

vernacular scenes depicted: the peasant woman going to market with her wares, the butcher busy slaughtering the calf, the spinner at her wheel, the policeman and the magistrate, all scenes the potter would have encountered in his own daily life, and very different from the forms, symbols and patterns evident in English pottery of the period.

The Langnau district was famous also for its production of the elaborate sucrières in the Rococo manner. These were given as marriage gifts and the lids were elaborately decorated (see page 103). They also made wonderful soup tureens, often covered with applied decoration in the form of carrots and fruit.

I know a charming castellated ink pot, and a cafetiere as well. Unusually, the spouts of these coffee pots are thrown or moulded as with English tea pots, rather than having a pulled lip. Often the lid is attached with a short metal chain to the handle.

The Glaisher Collection in the Fitzwilliam Museum, Cambridge, contains much of this ware, and it can be seen to be more delicate than the other continental wares.

Heimberg, latterly known as Thonne or Thun. Heimberg wares have a very distinctive, rich, red body, often covered or partly covered with a brown/black slip and trailed in white, sometimes painted with green (copper), yellow (antimony), orange slip and cobalt blue under a clear glaze.

There is a large group of plates trailed and scratched on a rich dark slip, almost chestnut in colour, with lively illustrated scenes such as horse and carriage, a lady with a rabbit for the pot, or a couple eating and talking at table. This work is easily recognizable by the lavish use of swags as a decorative motif, rather like elaborate curtain pelmets. There is a small group of coffee pots, flasks and sugar bowls that are decorated on an ivory coloured background with trailing, a little scratching and considerable use of cobalt. Coming at the beginning of the eighteenth century, and unlike much of the earlier work, although in no way similar to Delft it was perhaps made at a time when blue and white was particularly fashionable.

A coffee jug from Heimberg. 10″ high, 1820–40. White slip and sgraffito on brown body with slip and oxide painting.

Thonne (Thoune, Thun) continued producing slipwares, particularly trailed white on blue as well as more elaborate techniques, well into the twentieth century. There are as many as thirty-two potteries still working and their produce can be seen in a gallery in the town. The Castle Museum contains a small but lively collection of

Heimberg plate, 1840, with sgraffito and slip trailing on a black engobe. The inner rim shows the 'wasp' technique.

local slipwares, as well as work from other districts, in particular Langnau – 'Well worth a detour', to quote Michelin.

Spain

In Spain, oddly enough, there is no history of the type of lead-glazed sgraffito ware as seen in Germany and Italy, and, to a lesser extent, in France. Tin glaze was used from 1500 onward, but in the country potteries trailed slip was and is still used, principally white on a red body. The most decorative of these techniques can be found in **Alba de Tormes**, near Salamanca, where the filigree barrella is the most remarkable object made. This thrown barrel-type vessel, mounted on a cylindrical base and surmounted by an efflorescence of decorated clay strips, celebrates both the harvest and the potter's art – rather as do the brilliantly decorated gingerbread figures made by the bakers of eastern Europe. Wine jugs, salad bowls, flower pots and ornamental plates are also made in Alba de Tormes, all with a lovely, crisp, trailed application of white slip.

In **Ubeda**, Andalusia, some simple, rather rough wares are made, but often with a nice cockerel as decoration on plates. In **Prera**, Cataluña, they still make quantities of good, deep plates with two wide bands of white slip on the rim and, unusually, some plates with white interior slip and a circle of brown dots in the centre.

There are several interesting slipware potteries in Galicia, one of which is in **Buno**. Gorin Garcia makes simple functional pots, jugs, flat plates and bowls banded with white slip, both trailed and brushed. Some of the plates have a cross superimposed on a simple looped design; ungainly and unaesthetic, but looking as if the dish were used traditionally for some special Easter cake or other religious occasion.

Also in Galicia is the pottery of Lopez Lombado at **Bonxe**, where rather more sophisticated and touristic pots are made

Filigree barella and potter from Alba de Tormes.

although there is a great deal of variation in the forms and decoration, most of which is on a pale body. There are jugs, cantaros and an amusing jug in the form of a man with a little bird in his hand.

In the same town, Indaleno Lonbrogomez makes beautiful traditional jugs, lead-glazed on the inside and on the neck outside. The spouts are not very well defined and the strong handle descends from the rim to join the bulbous body. White slip is applied by brush to the body of the pots in two wide bands with broad arcs of white and two brushhead 'dots' under their rims. The red body has a wonderful toasted appearance, caused by the wood firing, giving the jug a timeless quality. A lifetime of throwing and decorating such jugs shows in their uncompromising and beautiful form, reflecting the potter's experience and instinctive judgement.

In **Extremadura**, simple well-shaped bowls and dishes are being made at Salvatierra de los Barros, splashed with copper and manganese. They produce fairly competent slip-trailed dishes, white on the red body, and a 'bottle' is also made with an unusual dome-shaped top. Unglazed red wares are produced in the same region, burnished into patterns with a pebble.

In **Andalusia** there is less lead-glazed pottery, as this area is the centre of majolica production, but in Lora del Rio there is one potter, Jose Monge, making globular bottles from a pinkish-brown body, coated in white slip which gives great luminosity to the uneven green copper glaze.

In **Albox**, Andalusia, two types of dishes are made, one coated with white slip with its rim painted in broad strokes of copper and manganese oxides, forming an interlaced, four-point star pattern. The other, made of yellow clay, has slip-trailed borders of five chevron motifs forming five-pointed star patterns around a central scroll. At **Nijar**, in the same State, some good splattered flat dishes are produced. Manganese, cobalt and copper mingle and separate on the white slip. **Palma del Rio** is a village with a potter appropriately named Handel, who decorates slightly more touristic forms with copper and pale manganese, but the trailing is assured and pleasant on a white ground.

In **La Mancha**, there are several potteries making traditional shaped jugs, cooking pans and lidded pots but with unimaginative trailing – white on the red body. However, one potter, Baltasar Moreno, decorates on a white slip ground using iron and a brightish green which looks more like cobalt than copper. The glaze is a pale honey colour and the whole effect is sophisticated and pleasant, partly because the forms are bold and assured.

In Cataluña there are several earthenware potters producing strongly banded pots of traditional shape. In spite of being near the Costa Brava, work from this area retains its integrity, although there are indeed other debased forms produced for the tourists. I have in my possession a cantaro, probably dating from the early twentieth century, with raised slip decoration almost like the barbotine technique. This is thrown in a white clay and trailed with a slip made from the same body clay.

White on white: barbotine-like trailing on a cantaro.

In conclusion, it is good to see in the latter part of the twentieth century, in a country whose economy is largely dependent on its holiday visitors, such a vast body of slip-decorated, lead-glazed earthenware, much of it traditional in form, although I doubt whether a great deal of it can be used for cooking in the old manner, on charcoal fires. Many English expatriates fill their houses with local craftwork and do seem to appreciate and admire the excellent workmanship, and this habit encourages a continuance of the craft.

Italy

One cannot discuss the pottery of Italy without reference to Majolica, the beautiful tin-glaze wares made from Renaissance times, especially in Deruta, Urbino and Faenza, this latter town lending its name to 'Faience'.

From the fifteenth century, earthenware in the style that Picolpaso described, 'questa pitture chiamasi sgraffio' ('this painting is called sgraffito'), in his manuscript *Li tre libri dell' Arte del Vasaio*, was widely made. There are dishes of this type in England in the Ashmolean Museum, the Victoria & Albert Museum, and also in the Wallace Collection where there is a fine dish 17 inches in diameter, dated between 1480 and 1500 and attributed to Bologna.

In the fifteenth and sixteenth centuries in other parts of Italy (possibly Urbino, Castello and Padua), stylized foliage patterns gave way to more elaborate decoration, but this method of decoration became more sketchy again towards the end of the sixteenth century as the majolica techniques were developed. With the increasing use of tin glaze for the gentry, the sgraffito decoration under a lead glaze enhanced with iron and copper, and occasionally manganese and cobalt, was used for 'country' wares. The body of these pots was a rich red and they were fired to 950°C.

Many fragments of Italian sgraffito dishes, very simply decorated with bands or a wheatsheaf rim design, were excavated in the famous Castle Street dig in Plymouth, England, as well as deeper bowls with surface slip marbling (report by the Plymouth City Museum

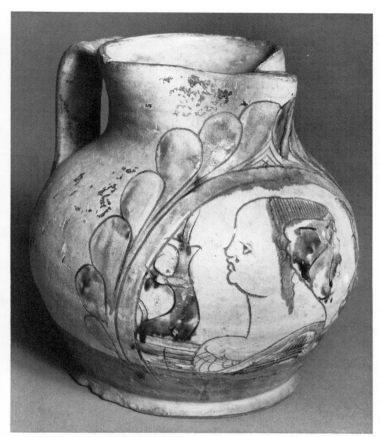

Jug with portrait head from Orvieto, 7″ high, late fifteenth century. Sgraffito through white engobe with painted manganese and copper, and a clear lead glaze.

and Art Gallery in 1979), showing that this lead-glazed ware was exported at an early date, though in smaller quantities than the tin-glazed albarellas, posset pots, ointment jars and large decorative plates.

The term *mezza-maiolica* has been used to describe a technique of scratching through a white slip into the body colour and enhancing with painted oxides at the leather-hard stage under the glaze, as opposed to surface painting used on the tin-glazed wares. This term *mezza-maiolica* is now in disuse, as it is considered to be confusing, but the technique is of interest to the contemporary potter and is discussed in detail in chapter 2.

One may summarize by saying that slipwares, as we understand them, were and are extremely rare in the mainland of Italy. In Sicily it is a different story.

Sicily

Ceramics have a long history in Sicily, with originally a strong Islamic influence, dating from their conquest in 827 AD.

From the fourteenth century, lustre techniques were used in a rather similar manner to the Italian majolica of the same period from Gubbio and Deruta. By the same date, a form of lead-glazed, slip-decorated pottery had emerged which continued to exist alongside the tin-glazed wares through the centuries. These pots were principally domestic functional pots. Undecorated oil lamps from **Coltesano** were the most remarkable, consisting of a kind of central etagère of one, two or three flat dishes in diminishing size around a central bottle-shape, surmounted by a top carrying handle. On each tier of this lumere there are between seven and fourteen small oil pots, each a simple dish about 2 inches in diameter with a pinched spout for

A large plate from the end of the fifteenth century, Bologna. Sgraffito through white engobe to red body, with some cut-out background and hatching, and painted in manganese and copper oxide. 17″ diameter.

the wick and all joined together by a top strap. It is very interesting to see an oil 'candelabrum', and as far as I know this is unique to Coltesano.

The bold water containers of **Burgio** continue to be made today in the eighteenth-century tradition, their strongly defined throwing marks accentuated by vivid copper and manganese oxide splattered on to the clear glaze. The body clay is a pale reddish-cream in colour. Oil lamps are also made in Burgio, and are unlike any others I know. They have the traditional pinched cup, but this is placed on a bottle-like pot with a broad gutter around its belly, presumably to catch any oil spillage. The handle springs from the base of the cup to the lower part of the bottle.

Caltagirone is well-known for its lovely big (24 inches high) honey-coloured container jars, decorated with brushed slip in greens, blues and browns. The lids of these straight-sided pots are pierced to prevent the dried beans that they contain from going mouldy. In this same village there are other potteries producing moulds for florentines (small cakes like madeleines) with religious motifs such as the Sacred Heart, a fish, and the pilgrim shell, inscribed into them. The Sicilian version of the Toby Jug, modelled with gentlemen's faces with applied hair and moustache, are also made in the same area. These have a good pouring lip and balanced handle in white and blue tin glaze. Puzzle jugs, bird whistles, pig money boxes and brandy flasks that are very similar to those made elsewhere on the continent also come from this district. The pots often have applied or roughly press-moulded decoration that is coloured with copper green slip. Holy water stoups are still made here in lead-glazed earthenware dipped in coloured slips, although the bulk of these are made in white tin-glaze elsewhere.

Oil lamps in other startling forms are made in **Santo Stefano**. These are many-handled and quite hideous, liberally splattered with strong copper and iron oxides almost metallic in effect. One of the most traditional Sicilian forms found here is the 'pigne' (the Mediterranean pine or 'piñon' that produces the edible pine kernels). Purely decorative, these moulded shapes, from 5 to 9 inches high, look very attractive on shelf or windowsill and are always one-coloured, either with green or yellow slip. Typical figurines made in the same village represent Saracen knights on surprised horses carrying off protesting ladies. These amusing statuettes are usually lead glazed on to the body colour, or have an orange slip under the glaze. All the lead-glazed work is once-fired with wood to about 980°C.

The folk art in Sicily is very rich, with nearly every object that moves or stands in the home covered in brilliant decoration depicting both sacred and profane subjects, the most famous of these artefacts being the cart, painted not unlike the traditional fairground carousel, the Sicilian work being carved in relief as well as coloured.

Now that the horse and cart is not used so frequently, other more modern forms of transport are decorated, the pick-up trucks often having wooden panelled bodies with elaborate scenes of Saracen battles painted in red, blue, yellow and green.

Puppet operas are taken round to the villages and the soldier dolls have wonderfully gilded and embossed armour. The decorative nature of these puppets is very similar to the flasks and figurines of the potters. It is rewarding and exciting to see so much of the traditional folk art forms still being made and appreciated by a population deeply involved with its religious and historic past.

In many respects, Sicily makes a contrast with England where lack of religious cohesion and earlier industrialisation brought an end to traditional folk art. Young artists studying old techniques – such as barge painting – are not working in a craft tradition, and many of these old trades (like thatching, wooden spoon carving and corn dolly making) have become middle-class interests even up to a professional level. The mariner's arts (like rope plaiting and knotting) are now bastardized as the macramé plant-holder.

Christian iconography is altogether richer, and many functional objects are made in Roman Catholic societies, as they always have been, for the church and home. The Christian iconography is rich in symbols such as the ass, the bee, the cock, the dove, the dragon or serpent representing the devil, and most frequently the fish. The five Greek letters forming the word 'fish' are the initial letters of the five words 'Jesus Christ God's Son Saviour' – I X O U G. The hare is not only the defenceless being, one who puts his trust in God, but also the symbol of lust and fecundity as is the horse. It is interesting that the owl is a figure of darkness and evil, often depicted at the scene of the crucifixion not, as we often think, as 'a wise old bird' but a trickster. The pelican is renowned as the bird who pierces its own breast to give its life's blood to its offspring, thus symbolizing Christ's sacrifice on the Cross. The shell – cockle or scallop – signifies pilgrimage, the unicorn was accepted as the symbol of purity in general and feminine chastity in particular.

In parenthesis, it may be said that many of these forms were utilized in the seventeenth century by Thomas Toft on his plates, showing his Roman Catholic heritage and his knowledge of religious iconography, particularly in his wonderful treatment of The Pelican in her Piety on a 20 inch charger. The owl, the unicorn, cockerels and fish appear also on other seventeenth-century potters' dishes.

Portugal

The most interesting slip-decorated pottery that I have come across in Portugal is from **Barcelos** in the north (Minho), about seventy kilometres north of Porto. Characteristic designs consist of compact patterns of white dots representing bunches of grapes, tulips, star motifs, etc. The body is a red earthenware, wood-fired, often with lovely blackish markings from the reduction firing. A traditional shape is the oval bowl used for rice cooking. There are also simple lidded casserole shapes and an interesting lidded jar with two strap handles and three strong, thrown legs. There are many dishes with upright sides, some decorated with lines as opposed to dots, many depicting fishes as well as cockerels, leaves, and a heart motif which is

Above **bird and feather, and,** *below,* **fish bowls. White slip trailing on red body from Barcelos. Modern.**

superimposed with a cross and may well be sacred.

All these pots are lead-glazed and the work is vigorously decorated on to the body without the intervention of a covering engobe. This allows the richness of the wood-fired clay to become an integral part of the design. Sometimes there are black smoke marks, almost like lace or a cloud traced over the body. This, and the low temperature firing, contributes to the final seductive appearance of the pots. Certainly in 1977 and 1978, when they were noted by Drs Angelika and Heinz Spielmann, these pots were bought by the locals for their use and were not specifically made for the tourists.

In **Beira**, central Portugal, in the first part of the twentieth century, shallow bowls approximately 9 inches in diameter were made, decorated on a white slip ground with brush and stencil work in blues, copper-green, manganese and ochre, and were somewhat Art Deco in feeling.

An immense amount of pottery, now both stoneware and earthenware, is made extensively in Portugal for the tourists, and it is encouraging to see that the slipware tradition continues alongside the majolica ware.

France

It is impossible to write about the lead-glazed earthenware of France without mentioning Bernard Palissy, and it is worth digressing to relate something of his extraordinary work and life. Born in the Lot et Garonne in 1499, he worked as portrait painter, glass-maker and surveyor until in about 1562 he invented a technique of moulding extraordinary rustic figurines and dishes, including snakes and toads moulded from the creatures themselves, together with flowers, applied in relief, the whole lead-glazed and coloured with manganese and copper. Some of these phenomena were created for Catherine de Medici. After sixteen years of experiments he developed the production of Faience in France. He lectured on

scientific subjects, wrote on philosophy, recognized the nature of fossil forms and held that water played a fundamental role in nature. He was banished to the Bastille as a Huguenot, and finally, at the age of ninety, he was hanged, strangled and burned for heresy on 4 July, 1589.

Whereas Palissy was a unique individual of great influence, the centre of activity in the development of French slipwares was undoubtedly the Beauvais area. The map below shows the main potteries in relation to both the old and new routes.

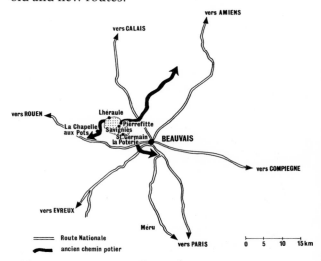

Old pottery centres near Beauvais.

The picture of conditions in the seventeenth- and eighteenth-century French potteries is much the same as in England, with similar large holes, 20–60 feet in depth, dug indiscriminately for the traveller to fall into. The huge mounds of clay beside the potteries were also unsightly and unsafe. Woods were destroyed for their fuel, and smoke poured from the kilns to the annoyance of many. For a stoneware firing, between sixteen and eighteen cords* of wood were used, and 400 faggots burned to reach the final temperature.

In April, when the frosts ceased, horses and donkeys led by the children went to the hills to collect clay, and this was later foot-wedged, while lead for the glaze was pounded by hand.

*A cord is $4 \times 4 \times 14$ feet of timber.

Continental slipwares

The glazed wares coming mainly from the Savignies potteries were transported via three main routes to Rouen, Paris and Amiens, first by pack horse and later by wagon.

The Beauvais potters formed a strong guild to protect their interests and were deeply involved in the life of their community. This is not the impression that one gathers of English potters in the seventeenth and eighteenth centuries.

On the 'Potters Feast Day' (which incidentally lasted three days) the potter gave a great repast for all his workers, combined with mass and a religious procession. A meal was given to the old and poor in the village on the third day. During the eighteenth century the potters were a microcosm of their society, but the traditions were sadly lost by the end of the nineteenth century. This comment of Claudine Cartier I think is worth repeating in the original: 'L'atmosphère gaie et joyeuse semble cependant en contradiction avec le caractère essentiellement religieux et sérieux d'une partie de la production'.

The slip-trailed work that has survived is principally plates and bowls, as well as alms dishes, sometimes described as 'double bowls' because of the small, thrown interior section.

Inspirational themes appear to have come from the Orient via Italy and Spain, as well as

Beauvaisis dish, 'mythical beasts', with tulip and rope design. 17″ diameter, 1674. White slip trailing on red engobe, honey glaze.

from Holland – hares, stags, stylized flowers and the tulip are frequently used. Lead glaze gave a rich life to pieces that were principally used as ornament.

There were few similarities in the seventeenth century between the French and English pots. The Staffordshire decorative Royalist subjects were unique to England, but some motifs, such as the tulip, were universal.

A group of work from the same region is religious in content, some unusual plates being decorated with an altar, monstrance and candlesticks, cunningly and charmingly contained in a kind of 'fish-bone' wreath.

Although there is some sgraffito work, apart from the unique double-slipped pots mentioned on page 57, it is not as elaborate or skilled as German work of the same periods (seventeenth/nineteenth centuries).

The hollow wares are often unusual in form and function, frequently being made for the Church: 'plats à quêter' (for collecting alms), 'bénitiers' (holy water stoups), or 'fontaines' (water-cisterns). There is also some evidence of Stations of the Cross being made as relief plaques. The bonus of religious commissions seldom came the way of the English potters.

The French hollow-wares of the seventeenth

Beauvaisis dish.

Continental slipwares

and nineteenth centuries are in principle very different from the English pots, being much to do with containing wine or oil, or specialized shapes for cooking regional dishes, but I have seen an illustration of one puzzle jug, this being very similar to the English. There are also looped, handled, sprigged and embossed pots so encumbered with loops and whorls that it is difficult to see a function, though they are not unlike some of the Burton-in-Lonsdale money boxes.

Where writing occurs on plates, it is often in the centre and in lower-case letters. I have not seen any wording as skilfully executed as that of Thomas Toft. One of the most interesting slipware dishes (of unknown origin) is in Sèvres Museum, and this is decorated in a combination of trailing and scratched techniques. Inscribed 'Roy 1688', it shows the King, mounted on his stallion, proudly waving his sword over his prostrate foe. This piece is the only one I know which bears some relationship to German wares, where the horse and soldier were a favourite theme.

Above detail from Beauvaisis plate showing soldier with pike, 1731. Sgraffito through white engobe with copper manganese and orange slip on red body. *Left* seventeenth-century French plate showing mounted king slaying a recumbent foe, with slip trailing and sgraffito in white engobe on a red body. The painting is in copper and manganese under a clear lead glaze.

Continental slipwares

In the sixteenth century the work known as Saint-Porchaire is interesting but limited, being covered with a clear glaze on to the ivory coloured body and decorated in brown or black, but the technique of this decoration is not understood. The clay is very similar to that of Saintes, although much of the sixteenth-century ware from here was moulded and embossed with coats of arms and glazed in a rich copper green. There are ovoid flasks and pitchers with a double form, the outer being pierced.

In the seventeenth century a group of lead-glazed reddish-brown wares is attributed to Avignon. These pots are rather in the Italian style and the forms were inspired by metal work. There is a charming fountain dated 1786 from **Ligron** (Sarthe) which has a great deal of applied decoration in white clay on to the red body. Camels, elephants, trees and leaves are captured on this interesting pot. The bowl is shell shaped and contains frogs and cray-fish in high relief, after Palissy. The whole piece is topped by a portrait figure 'Guemonneau de la Forteries', surgeon at Courcelles, near Ligron. The fountain is $18\frac{1}{2}$ inches high and the bowl $13\frac{1}{4}$ inches in diameter, and it can be seen in the Musée de Ceramique, Sèvres.

Vallauris in the south, known now as the place where Picasso fashioned his pots, has always been a pottery centre with a long tradition of making cooking pots, as well as some simple slip-trailed wares.

Avon, near Fontainbleu, produced little pottery figurines around 1620 and **Manerbe** in Normandy specialized in making roof finials. This tradition continues, although with salt glaze on red earthenware or a sort of simulated salt glaze effect produced with a fine lustrous chestnut-coloured slip. A pottery dove is the most common form to be seen on rooftops.

Alsatian wares

Alsace Lorraine is one of the few regions where slipwares continue to be made in the traditional way. This area of pine forests, large farms and freezing winters specializes in the making of sweetmeats and cakes. For this purpose, the famous gügelhopf and gingerbread moulds are made. In earlier times they were left rough outside and beautifully finished inside. Nowadays they are used as wall ornaments and are often decorated outside as well. Also, the old gingerbread forms have been utilized as moulds by the potters. These make very decorative plaques and are an excellent medium for slip trailing as this bears some resemblance to icing and makes the 'gingerbread people' look very authentic.

Slipwares are produced now by several small factories as well as a few individual potters. Much of the work is jiggered and jolleyed, but it is all hand-decorated and most of the pots are strictly functional, as well as being so bright and pleasing to the eye. Coffee sets, gratin dishes, soup tureens and casseroles are the most common wares now made. The traditional background colour for most of the cooking ware is a rich chestnut brown, with flowers and leaves trailed in white, chrome green and orange slips under a clear glaze. I have in my possession a magnificent large casserole in just these colours, similar in form to the classic French red earthenware type, but made more beautiful by the decoration. The body of these Alsace wares is white and this is one of the reasons why the colours appear so brilliant.

Two country jugs, c. 1910, from the South of France, with white engobe on white body and slip trailing. In the foreground, an Alsace Lorraine cream jug, trailed in green and white over reddish-brown engobe on white body. All clear glaze.

Lidded jar by Claire Bogino with slip trailing.

Alsatian ware is available everywhere in the region in china shops and in the country markets. It is functional, easy on the eye and pleasant in use: the best way to understand the excellence of form and decoration. There are not many places where slipwares are so readily available in such pleasing forms.

Slip-trailed decoration was used on country pots throughout France, particularly in the south. I have mentioned in the chapter on historic slip-trailed wares the work from the **Saintes** area – la Chapelle des Pots – some of it ornamental in the sense of applied decoration. Work can be seen in the La Rochelle Museum (Charente) but, as in England, the best pots are in the national rather than the provincial museums. It is well worth visiting the Musée Departmental de l'Oise in Beauvais and the Musée National de Ceramique in Sèvres.

Contemporary slipware in France

In France, as in Italy, lead-glazed earthenware was largely superseded by tin-glazed wares. Nevertheless, it is interesting to note that there are some contemporary potters, notably Paul Salmona and Claire Bogino (from St Chaptes, near Nimes), producing lovely slip-decorated pots but on predominantly oriental forms.

Paul Salmona says, 'What interests me and excites my curiosity the most is that unobtrusive but very ancient rapport between clay and the act of writing, between clay and the written word.' Although no readable language is trailed on his lovely pots, the sensitive lines are calligraphic in essence (see page 104).

He uses a sanded red earthenware clay and has two firings after the slip-trailed decoration, a bisque and a glost firing to 1000°C. The bottle-type kiln takes one ton of wood for the glost firing which lasts nine hours, a strong reducing atmosphere being induced one hour before completion of the firing. A white clay from Bresse is used for the slip, and the different colours are obtained by adding 4 per cent of iron for the red, 4 per cent of copper for the green, and 20 per cent manganese for the brown. Cobalt is not used.

Salmona is lucky enough to be able to glaze with raw lead, as distinct from the non-toxic fritted lead glazes required by law in other countries today. The effect on his work is lovely, with patches of oxidation on the reduced pot. The use of lead gives Salmona's work a particularly rich and varied texture and colour, whether he is decorating on the white or the black slip

Claire Bogino works with Salmona, using the same clay, glaze and kiln. Her slips are more varied, with random splashes of green and fine black trailing. She deforms her work, sometimes notching it with a stick, and her philosophy is altogether more abstract than Salmona's: 'For me the interest lies not in what the object contains, nor in its colour, nor in its technical qualities, for all that is secondary; but in the object as image, the object as enigma.' Nevertheless, the work I have seen is definitely usable.

Belgium

The principal pottery district in Belgium is **Thorout**, near Bruges, where earthenware for local distribution has been made since the eighteenth century. These objects are particularly charming, the glaze being a bright butter-yellow. Many of the pots were like toys, exemplified by the 7 inch high model armoire in the Fitzwilliam Museum, Cambridge, where there is also a watch pocket. The decoration is applied on to a white background and coloured with orange and turquoise slips – a most unusual colour. Much of the decoration is in relief, employing formalized leaves and flowers.

The particular wares in question date from the late eighteenth century to the early part of the twentieth century.

Slip trailing, sgraffito and relief decoration united on pintes (1 pint) 'Miska' Toby Jugs, 1848, by Mihály Rajszy.

Hungary

Hungarians were originally a semi-nomadic people. In medieval Hungary, pottery was unglazed, sometimes slip-painted. It was only in the late fifteenth century that glaze began to be used, beginning with green stove tiles and then vessels.

During the Osman-Turkish occupation in the sixteenth/seventeenth centuries, slip-trailed dishes decorated in black, red and green under a transparent glaze were made in many districts. The most splendid seventeenth-century piece to survive is three feet in diameter, decorated on a white background with a formalized vase of 'flowers', including some tulip shapes. This can be seen in the National Ethnographic Museum in Budapest. The tradition of slip-trailing continued into the nineteenth century, with the forms becoming more elaborate, often with the inclusion of sgraffito techniques, principally under a pale honey or copper-green glaze. Large jugs made for the various guilds had applied decoration as well as the scratched wording.

Various towns in Hungary renowned for their

Wine jug by Mihály Nagy junior from Tiszafured, 1840. Sgraffito and slip trailing on white engobe.

pottery include **Szekszard** in western Hungary, **Tiszafured**, **Hodmezovasarhely**, **Mezotur**, **Siklos** and **Karcog**, where in the present day the famous old master Kántor Sándor still works.

The principal forms of Hungarian pottery are similar to those in many eastern European countries: wall plates as used in all peasant societies for decoration, lipless jugs or bocaly used for wine and large jugs used for water with a strainer fitted into the neck of the pot below the lip.

Brandy flasks were also made by flattening the round thrown bottle into an oval between two boards. These had inscriptions very similar to our English harvest jugs, such as 'Drink round my jovial fellows', etc., and at the time of the Hapsburg domination they were beautifully decorated in red and black slips, and depicted a Hussar on his prancing horse. The mikail (miska) was a large wine jug sometimes three feet tall, in the form of a man, equivalent to the English Toby Jug. All these traditions have been revived and encouraged under the communist regime, where 'people's art' as opposed to 'fine art' is supported with local pottery competitions.

Romania

In many ways it is difficult to separate Romanian from Hungarian work, especially as the boundaries have changed.

In Transylvania there were no glazed pots made by Romanian potters, but unglazed wares were made in the eighteenth century and some are still being made in the following districts: **Horezu-Pesti**, **Craiova**, **Timisoara**, **Oradea**, **Baia Mare**, **Suceava**, **Hune Doara**, **Sibin**, **Ardeal**, **Hargnita**.

The best Transylvanian glazed ware was either Saxon (many complex eighteenth-century pieces of slip-trailed and brush-painted wares were often white and blue), or Hungarian. One group is from the Surer region.

The Romanian ware outside Transylvania is very interesting, as there is a great deal of combed, sgraffito and slip-trailed work. The designs on the whole appear to be simpler, more floral and more geometric than the Hungarian pots with their birds and people, but in the mountains, stags are the principal motif on plates.

The walls of Romanian homes are covered in

Large slip-trailed dish from northern Hungary, seventeenth century. White slip ground, dark brown slip-trailed outlines with red, green and yellow colouring under clear glaze. On the reverse side is the incised coat-of-arms of Hungary. 36″ diameter.

Stork and Lily of the Valley dish. White and copper-green slip trailing on pale red engobe from Slovakia. A gift to a new mother. 14″ diameter.

pots when not hung with rich 'scoarte' (wall carpets). The Village and Folk Art Museum in Bucharest has a magnificent collection of this work, and some can also be seen in the Horniman Museum in London.

Slovakia

Slipwares were, and are still produced in several areas. **Sobotiste** was producing honey glazed ware in the nineteenth century. This was decorated with copper and these dishes often have the trellis pattern on the rim.

In the hamlet of **Pozdisovce** they made dishes and trailed with white, copper and orange slips on to the red body in a simple but decorative way, generally not using figurative motifs.

Pukanec was known for its marbling techniques, as was **Modra**. Black and white slips were trailed on to the bright orange body in an unsubtle but attractive way.

Sebranice, near Litomysl, made lipless jugs that were scratched through the white slip on to a red ground and often with the background cut away. The work in Sebranice is definitely more sophisticated than in most other regions.

In the village of **Trstena**, in the earlier part of this century, the potters were trailing with

black on to a white background, using also the sgraffito technique.

Much of the Slovakian work is lively and the peoples have a rich and varied Folk Art tradition, particularly in carved and painted wood and Icon-like paintings on glass. As is well known, their glass was at one time among the most famous in the world and there was a very efficient export trade.

As happened in many other countries, tin glaze was employed in the eighteenth century, and many wine jugs similar to the Haban wares of Hungary were painted in a very lively manner.

Slip-decorated and lead-glazed pots continued to be made alongside the majolica, and the tradition continues to the present time.

Poland

This country is an important source of domestic slipware, emanating from many regions. **Bialystok**, **Lublin**, and **Kielce** are the most noteworthy areas where pottery has been and continues to be made. The **Ilza** district has excellent stoneware clay, and pottery has been made with this material since the sixteenth century, but the weekly market in Ilza is also full of colourful earthenware produced in the same area, particularly models of chapels, nativities and village life. Children's whistles in the form of dogs, houses and birds are also very popular. Another speciality is the well known turkey with its tail spread out to make a wonderful circular shape.

It is interesting to see in Roman Catholic countries such as Poland the richness of their source material. Holy water stoups, shrines and small figures of saints were also popular. The museum in Rabka organized a competition for rural nativity crib groups in 1967, allied to competitions for companies to produce pageants connected with winter and spring rites. Most of the companies ignored the pagan aspects, and presented Christmas plays – the so-called live nativity cribs.

A great deal of unglazed, coarser pottery is made in the villages of **Katy**, **Szczekociny** and **Dankow**, but with a stoneware clay.

Continental slipwares

Polish slipware. *Below* fine spiral slip trailing in white on red body, late nineteenth century, from Ciche. *Right* sgraffito through white engobe to red with copper painting on a twentieth-century flask from Sokl (now Ukraine). *Bottom left* fish-scale pattern slip trailing in white and orange on black engobe from Gdansk region, 1930s, and, *bottom right* red slip-trailed hens on white engobe from Tazek Ordywacki Tarnobrzeg region. Modern.

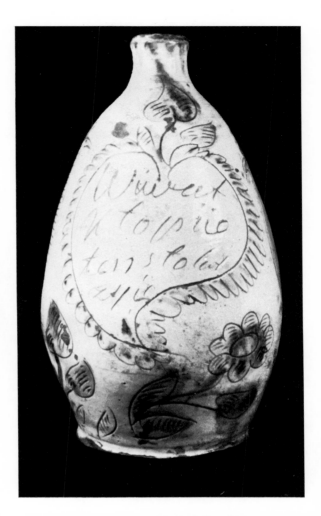

Continental slipwares

Sokolów, Malapolski, Wyszków, Cezajsk and the court potteries of **Miechocin** in the second half of the nineteenth century recommended the making of slip-decorated wares, when people in small towns and villages started to show a renewed interest. This changed the rustic methods of working and mass production became popular, necessitating a simplified form of decoration. Generally speaking, plant motifs become the most commonplace. In the Kurpe region, geometric motifs were employed, and in **Bochnia** the plates were decorated with a single female figure, which was unusual.

In the Miechocin region, decoration was bold, often with white slip-trailing on a black background, using the 'fish tail' pattern. In the eastern regions of Poland the oldest traditions are present, with unglazed pots for everyday use, as glazing was expensive. In this area they specialized in making earthenware pots to contain liquids. In **Lodyszki**, carrying and measuring jugs were made, as were cooking pots, eating bowls, and double-pots used to carry food to the workers in the fields.

The first potters in Miechocin were Huttites (Haban), working in tin glazes, as in Hungary. In the seventeenth century there were twelve workshops, but by the eighteenth century, with the fashionable popularity of the Delft wares, production began to decline and by the end of the eighteenth century the local registers show only bricklayers, no potters at all being recorded.

White slipped pottery continued in only a few centres, the most important being **Lażek Ordynaki** in the Janòw Lubelski district, a kind of folk semi-majolica. They also made combed ware, but scratched on the raw body, not through a slip. Stamped patterns, a kind of sprig decoration and the roulette wheel were other methods of decoration, as was the brush. A clay vessel with quill, or a cow-horn with quill, were used as trailing vessels, but most interesting of all was the 'spoon' method, where a tablespoon had its sides hammered upright into a long, narrow shovel-shape, and was used to pour a thick slip decoration in leaf forms on to a leather-hard pot. Sgraffito decorating through

the black slip to the pale body had nearly ceased in the nineteenth century. This story has been repeated so often throughout Europe: the advent of enamel ware, stoneware and faience caused the demise of rural potteries. In England it was the Staffordshire factory-made white wares that were the main competition to the rural pottery. Surprisingly, in Poland in the late nineteenth century, some potteries started up again producing traditional forms, but these were for a different customer – the town dweller.

Chmielno, Kartuzy in the Gdańsk region and **Czarnawies** in Bialystok were the main centres. They produced clay toys which were no longer for children but for adults, and figurines so elaborate as to be almost art objects. These were made in Ilza in the Radom region.

Potters in **Kielce** were making unusual sgraffito wares in the nineteenth century, while in the **Lublin** and **Kartuzy** regions grey burnished pots were still made alongside the slip-decorated production. Rzeszów was famous for its beautiful, plain black bottles of various shapes, covered with a transparent glaze over the black slips.

In **Chmielno** in the Kassubian district a family of potters, the Necel family, was slip trailing with traditional motifs, such as the lilac cluster, star, wreath, lily and fish scale. In **Sievadz** district, jugs were the speciality, nicely slip-trailed in white on to the rich red body. These pots were popular as they were waterproof: it must be remembered that earthenware is porous by nature, and not all pottery in Poland was glazed both inside and out because of the cost.

The **Kurpie** district is known for its large, slender jugs, covered in copper-green slip, enhanced with white slip-trailing. In a previous era these were used for oil storage. They also made big honey jars here: before the ready accessibility of sugar and its consequent low price, honey was the only sweetening agent, and most peasants would have had one or two beehives along with their cow and pig, and honey jars would have been commonplace. Incidentally, the Staffordshire version of the honey pot can be seen in both the Fitzwilliam

Right **Lily of the Valley dish from Upper Austria, eighteenth century, 14″ diameter, and,** *below* **two marriage gift sugar bowls from Langnau in Switzerland, slip-trailed and painted in antimony and copper, 1820.**

(Cambridgeshire) and Stoke-on-Trent Museums: these are particularly ornate, globular, one-handled pots, with a handsome lid.

Since the fourth century, burnished black pots ('siwaki'), have been made in **Biala Podlaska**, often decorated with sgraffito motifs. This tradition flowered in the nineteenth century and has continued in many other areas throughout the country. Kashubian pots are also black-burnished and these are made in the Kartuzy district. The shapes are somewhat different from the Biala pots, being similar to large globular Hungarian water pitchers – these forms occur throughout the Slovak regions and they are interesting as river or spring water containers, the neck being very narrow and opening out into a wider mouth which is filled with a pierced strainer. Cut-out clay circles are allowed to remain loose in the body of the pot: these rattle around and thus keep the interior clean, much as glass sherry decanters are cleaned with gunshot. The handle of these pitchers is always hollow and has a nipple through which the water is drunk.

Bolimów, a village near Nieborow in the Lowicz region, has a long tradition of pottery making, and until fairly recently there were at least twelve potters working here. Now there is only one man, Stefan Konopczynski, together with his sister, producing great globular jugs with sparse slip-trailed floral motifs on a cream or red background. These two potters are the fourth generation of the Konopczynski family continuing the tradition.

Slipwares are also made in the Mazovian and Pomeranian regions, and fortunately, although many of the traditional forms such as water pitchers, milk jugs and food carrying containers are not used for their original functions they are bought increasingly as decorative objects in the home, so the elaborate slip-trailing skills of Poland can be passed on to the next generation of potters.

Lidded vase by Paul Salmona, 20″ high. The varied coloration of the orange/green background is the result of wood-firing.

Conclusion

It is interesting that Claire Bogino, the French potter, says, 'Pottery today no longer fulfils a specific functional need.' This is absolutely true. It is a comment which I, too, have often used, and it must bear the responsibility and also be the rationalization for the mass of sculptural and abstract ceramic forms that are fashionable now. Nevertheless, there are many people who still love to hold and use unique hand-made objects. As a plea for functional ware of individuality and character I would mention that in the 1980s, when so many people have formalized kitchen units making the atmosphere horrendously clinical, it is even more important to have in one's environment hand-made bowls and plates, each of which has a certain fitness for a particular type of food. Equally, each pot holds within its structure the signature of the potter who made it.

It is always intriguing when studying the pottery from another culture to try and understand why tin-glaze has superseded the lead-glazed earthenwares. In certain areas it might be postulated that climate has some bearing on the manufacture – for slip-decorated wares have to be kept moist during decoration – but then why, for instance, in Sicily and Portugal do elaborate slipwares continue to be made? Perhaps it has less to do with climatic conditions than with communication, levels of sophistication and fashion trends.

It is essential for the modern potter to look at the folk art of other countries, as this helps us to place seventeenth-century and later slipware potters in their true perspective. Paintings were not available to poorer country folk, neither were tapestries or painted wall hangings. There does not seem to be much evidence of interior walls being painted in modest homes. Indeed, it is difficult to see how those people working every daylight hour could have found the time or energy to decorate their walls, but they *did* have colourful pottery to display on the shelf or dresser. In Britain a fashion for wall plates has never developed. In the early twentieth century the Staffordshire factories produced a white moulded plate with an open-slotted rim for ribbon threading and this was hung inside the canal boats. The central decoration consisted of roses, rural or village landscapes, and sometimes suitable mottoes. In many countries the need for decoration in the house was satisfied by these plates, and the associated painted wooden shelf with its protective plate rail with pegs underneath for jugs or cups. Likewise the English dresser had grooves to support many plates, which must have shone out in the dark and smokey kitchens, often rooms that did not have a chimney, only a smoke hole. The rich yellow of honey-glazed pots must have looked well on the plank tables, just as today they enliven the modular kitchen.

Most traditional pots would not have been fired much above 980°C and so were easily broken. Many rural pots in many different countries bear the legend 'This pan is made of earth – when it breaks the potter laughs.'

9
Clay and the written word

To the slipware potter, the written word is very important as writing on pots is a skill that he has developed in both the trailed and scratched techniques.

In my own work, at a time when folk art decoration was not fashionable, the words sold the pots. Equally, various nineteenth century and early twentieth century potteries recognized this. For instance, Buckley, near Chester, trailed 'BEEF' or 'PIE' into the bottom of their baking dishes, making these simple forms unique to their pottery and endearing to the customer.

Potteries such as Dicker and Chailey in Sussex, southern England, using their metal printers' type with an inlay technique, pressed gift inscriptions into costrels, tobacco jars and other commemorative pots. This was not unskilled work, and the resulting message looked very untidy unless the type was applied with mathematical precision on to an incised line. Hard metal type is not relaxed, and this informality is essential for the verse and humour that appeared on the Devon wares, where the sgraffito technique is ideally suited to a flowing hand – provided always that the clay is caught just in the right condition. If it is too wet, the tool gouges a deep channel in the clay and leaves a rough raised line. If the pot is too dry, a very sharp tool is needed and this makes a very fine and often static impression, as well as slowing down the work.

The various North Devon potteries, and particularly those in Bideford, made full use of 'The Word' and their great harvest jugs contain both presentation inscriptions and free verses.

These are placed all over the pot to balance the other incised decorations. The background is cut away on the North Devon pots to reveal the ships and tulips and other motifs in low relief. This is laborious work, and I am sure the potter was glad to leave large white-slipped areas where he could quickly scratch in the words that would make his individually ordered pot not only more interesting, but also worth more.

The South Devon potteries, as already stated, made a speciality of these incised sayings on their pots well into the mid twentieth century, and this technique was imitated, in most instances poorly, by other potteries throughout England, Scotland and Wales.

I find that the 'old saws' used in the South Devon wares are rather uninspiring and I have been unable to bring myself to use many of these words in my own work, whereas the inscriptions on North Devon pots are full of humour and originality.

Ewenny ware from Wales has quite a different feel, the scratched patterns being tighter and smaller and the background not cut away. They are also inscribed with very emotive lines, very nationalistic in flavour, such as 'Wales for ever'. Most of these particular pots date back to the turn of the century.

Donyatt in Somerset, although producing much of the earliest sgraffito wares, did not use words on those seventeenth-century pots. Apart from the fact that the tradition of the written word appears not to have existed in this area, it is evident that to be able to write was a rare skill. There is a tendency to assume that many of the rustic potters in this same period,

When I was in my Native place I was
a lump of Clay and digged was out of the Earth
and brought from thence away but now I am a jug
Became by Potters Art and Skill and now your
Servent am become and carry Ale I will
Jovial fellows Drink about Weel have more
When this is out

Mʳ Jⁿ FISHER.
COURT·BARTIN
YARNSCOMB
1795

Detail of
the inscription
under the harvest
jug illustrated on
page 60.

although perhaps putting a date or a name on a pot, were barely literate. If this were the case, then I can imagine there must have been great pride in the production of any written work, and admiration by the recipients who were, perhaps, unable to read themselves.

In the later nineteenth century, after the Industrial Revolution, when compulsory schooling was introduced, copy-books were printed and 'good' handwriting was universally taught.

In the nursery school in the late 1920s, copy-books were common, and many people of my generation write, if not beautifully, with a kind of casual elegance. Messages on pottery vary from the copper-plate to the inappropriate italic, but the best kind of lettering on a pot sits comfortably on the clay, and irregularity is not necessarily a disadvantage.

The written word on the pot performed multifarious functions, giving several different kinds of pleasure as well as enabling the potter to demonstrate not only his throwing skills but his educational achievement, and the price charged for these pots would be greatly in excess of that charged for the ordinary production wares.

The role of the potter in his community was a lowly one. He was a dirty man who created mess and confusion around him. His kilns belched smoke, his casual clay digging created havoc on the highways, sometimes lethal. With inscribed ware, his status was improved, and made his work much in demand in the nineteenth century for local dignitaries to use as presentation pots. Prizes for bowling, flower festivals, carnivals and other jollifications were popular. At a later date, there was a demand for individual commemorative pots for the opening of new factories, schools and hospitals, mayoral functions and royal presentations. The advent of transfer, and later silk screen methods, used in the Staffordshire potteries put paid to much of the bulk orders for mugs and other small gifts – as it does to my own – but the individually inscribed presentation piece was and is still a satisfying and successful enterprise.

Across Europe, 'writing' was used from the sixteenth century, both in the trailed and sgraffito manner, even if only to record the date and maker's initials in the central design of a plate. It is sad that the use of trailed lettering has been so limited on English pots. This, I am sure, is because it is technically so difficult, and to achieve an even flow of slip without blodges and splatters needs a great deal of skill and practice.

Switzerland, the birthplace of tourism, produced a rash of souvenir wares lettered with district names, although the eidelweiss as a design itself spells Switzerland to even the most untravelled collector. The German, French and Italian cantons each had, and still have, their own tradition and in Thun, for instance, the name is always clearly written on the base of the pot as well as the design number and potter's initials. The inscriptions on the Heimberg dishes are slip-trailed on the rim in lower-case letters, quite unlike the English style which was only in capitals.

In seventeenth-century France, sgraffito wares invariably contained useful and evocative inscriptions, and similar sentiments are expressed throughout Europe on country wares and also on the larger and more important pieces, such as those made in the eighteenth

A 'Hop-ware' wedding dish by William Watson, with applied decoration, from Belle Vue, Rye. 17″ diameter. Late nineteenth-century.

century in Germany in the Lower Rhine area.

I have collected together sayings from pots made in many different countries, and often the words in different languages carry the same message, especially those that apply to the potter and his clay, 'I am earth and so are you become', or 'Die Pfanne ist aus Erde gemacht, wer sie zerbricht, def Häfner lacht'. This sort of thing recurs literally hundreds of times on English and German pots.

It is difficult to decide how best to categorize the various sayings, and some of the inscriptions are clumsy in translation although fine in the original. There are political, nationalist and satirical sayings; there are phrases for presentation gifts; there are the many comments on females from virginal maids to cranky old wives. There is a group of Pennsylvanian German/Dutch nineteenth- and twentieth-century inscriptions that seem almost like direct speech. There are boozy words for large jugs, puzzle tyg and puzzle jug verses and wise sayings. There are also pots with religious inscriptions, from the few seventeenth-century Metropolitan wares to the many eighteenth-century North Rhine dishes. It has to be said that a phrase short enough to be inscribed on a

Jug with sgraffito decoration through white engobe to an agate body under a clear glaze, from north Staffordshire, inscribed to George Benteley 1779.

109

pot needs to be particularly wise, funny or apt to stand the test of time.

By studying the inscriptions, a pattern of social history emerges. Some pots were used in fact as political broadsheets, others as an outpouring of the potter's frustration with his daily life, many were simply traditional sayings that were retained as they were popular and sold well. Even if a pot is not dated and is inscribed, it is fairly easy to arrive at an indication if not of the political situation, at least of the period and often the potter's feelings at the moment of making the pot.

I know myself that I have often chosen what appears to me to be either an amusing or profound short poem to put on my jugs, but if these do not sell I am unable to use them again and must go back to the words that have been found to be the most popular such as 'This little jug in friendship take and keep it for the giver's sake.'

The best-known sayings scratched on to English pots are the motto wares of the Torquay potteries, first produced by Aller Vale during the last ten or fifteen years of the nineteenth century. This style was taken up in the present century by the other Torquay potteries and eventually became the typical bread-and-butter product of the local industry. This was characterized by having a little rhyme, precept, or longer quotation scratched through the cream-coloured ground on one side of the article, while the opposite side was usually decorated with what was known locally as 'scandy'. (The word 'scandy' has never been seen in print, and is variously pronounced by old pottery workers as 'scandee', 'scanda', or 'scandoo'.) The usual scandy pattern (page 56) consisted of a symmetrical arrangement of brush strokes and spots done in coloured slips, rather like an elaborate Prince of Wales's Feathers. Comparison with the picture on page 72 suggests a stylized development of an 'old Rhodian' motif. However, the word 'scandy' is said to be a corruption of 'Scandinavian', because the style of the painting resembles that found on traditional Norwegian furniture and known as 'rosemaling' (rose painting).

Mottoes were also provided on articles

decorated with the 'Abbotskerswell' daisy pattern (see page 56, left), but these were usually finished with an amber glaze, whereas the scandy ware always has a relatively colourless glaze.

It has been said that the inscriptions on early motto ware were always done in normal English and that, later, an exaggerated Devonshire dialect was adopted to appeal to the tourist trade. But, in fact, the mottoes were chosen more or less at random from a large repertoire, and a visitor who described the Aller Vale pottery at the end of the nineteenth century noted only one West Country motto amongst all those he saw at the Works. These mottoes (and this holds good for all the other Torquay firms) are always written in lower-case letters, and are never joined up as in normal writing script. Although the style of the printing is generally the same for all the potteries, the characteristic formation of some of the letters often makes it possible to associate articles with a certain pottery on the basis of handwriting.

The majority of small pieces made at Aller Vale had a design in slip on one side and a motto scratched through the slip on the other. Some of the mottoes were just a couple of words, others were as long as four or even six lines of verse. These generally expressed the Victorian virtues of hard work and sober living, in a lighthearted rather than a pious manner.

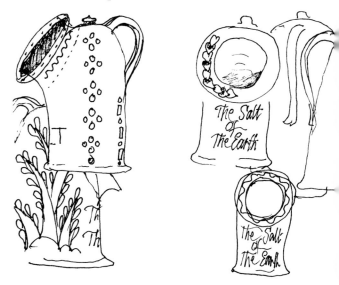

DO THE WORK THAT'S NEAREST,
THOUGH ITS DULL AT WHILES;
HELPING, WHEN YOU MEET THEM,
LAME DOGS OVER STILES.

It is interesting that at Aller Vale only one person was employed at one time to scratch the mottoes. This is in contrast to Collard's pottery at Poole in Dorset, where all of the girl decorators were allowed to do this work. Furthermore, at Aller Vale, with occasional exceptions, only two handwritings appear during the life of the pottery. The first handwriting which appears on early pieces only (normally red clay ware with unglazed bases), shows a somewhat introverted character, the writing leans backwards slightly, the letters are scratched thickly and are rather fuzzy in appearance. The second hand appears around 1890, and continues to the closure of the Aller Vale pottery in 1924. Many of the workers, including the motto scratcher, were then transferred to Watcombe pottery and the same handwriting can then be found on Watcombe pieces for a few years thereafter. This is a very attractive hand, scratched deep into the clay, with rather fancy capital letters – it is no wonder that this worker kept the job for so many years.

Some of the small items bear messages rather than mottoes, and were probably meant to be sent to distant friends or relatives as a present-cum-postcard. Examples of these messages are:

COME AN' ZEE US IN THE ZUMMER (a quotation from William Barnes.)

WHERE BE YOU NOW, DEAR? (a quotation from Thomas Hardy.)

IN FRIENDSHIP'S NAME, etc.

and they appear on useful items such as small jugs, vases and cream bowls.

TO A FRIEND'S HOUSE THE ROAD IS NEVER LONG (Watcombe pottery)

Thomas Hardy produced a special series of mottoes for the pottery, drawn from his Wessex novels, which were used on a range of pottery known as 'Hardy Ware.' One jar in this series represents the story of Gabriel Oak and bears the motto:

TO HIS SCORNFUL LOVE COMES GABRIEL OAK
AND ASKS TO BE ONE OF HER SHEPHERD FOLK

Any comprehensive list of inscriptions, even in a single language, would be rather tedious and very long. I am therefore appending a selected list, arranged systematically under categories.

South Devon Ware

NOW GOO AWAY YOU
CRABBED, JEALOUS CHAP
YOU SHAN'T KISS ME YOU SHAN'T
I'LL GI'YE A SLAP

AN' AS FOR KISSEN
O' – ME IF HE DID, I
DIDDEN AX'EN' TO, NOR
ZAY HE MID

BLESSED ARE THE DROWSY
FOR THEY SHALL SOON DROP OFF

(Candlestick)

MANY ARE CALLED BUT VEW GET UP.

(Candlestick)

SNORE AND YOU SLEEP ALONE

(Candlestick)

DON'T WORRY AND GET WRINKLES,
SMILE AND HAVE DIMPLES.

(Watcombe)

HELP YOURSELF. NOBODY'S LOOKING!

(Aller Vale)

IF YOU'VE GOT THE PIP, DON'T SQUEAK

(Watcombe)

IF YOU CAN'T BE AISY, BE AS AISY AS YOU CAN.

DAWNT'EE BE FOUND OUT NOW!

(Longpark)

DINNA SCALE THE CREAM

LITTLE DUTIES STILL PUT OFF
WILL END IN NEVER DONE,
BYE-AND-BYE IS SOON ENOUGH
HAS RUINED MANY A ONE

(Watcombe)

STEAL NOT THIS
POT FOR FEAR OF SHAME
FOR HERE YOU SEE

Clay and the written word

Old Saws

EVERYBODY IS HIS OWN NEAREST HEIR
I WILL ENJOY MYSELF BEFORE I DIE
(North Germany)

I AM THE BIRD OF ALL THINGS WHOSE BREAD I EAT
   WHOSE SONG I SING
(North Germany)

YOU CAN LIVE WITH A LOT BUT YOU HAVE TO LIVE
   WITH A LITTLE
(Turingen, Germany)

EVERY ONE LOVES YOUNG WOMEN AND OLD MONEY
(Odenwald)

S M
ONE
BURD IN
THE HAND
IS WORTH
TWO IN THE
BUSH
1726

(Malkin, impress moulded, Staffordshire)

BE MERY AND WIE
(Metropolitan pot)

GET OFF YOUNG BOY
BEWARE OF CERTAIN WOMEN AND MUCH SWEET
   WINE
(Langnau, Switzerland)

A MAN'S THOUGHTS AND HIS WISHES AND HIS
   CARE ONLY GO TOWARDS MONEY
(Simenthal, Switzerland)

LIKE THE LION, KING OF THE ANIMALS
THE FATHER OF THE HOUSE SHOULD RULE THE
   SERVANTS
(Switzerland)

DO NOT TRY TO CHANGE OTHER PEOPLE
STAY THE SAME AS YOU ARE
DO NOT BUILD YOUR HOPES ON YOUR FRIEND
DO NOT TRUST EVERYBODY — LOOK TO YOURSELF
DO NOT BE TOO PARTICULAR
(Swiss butter churn)

WHATEVER I DO
IT IS ALWAYS WRONG

AS A MAN LIVES SO SHALL HE DIE
AS A TREE FALLS SO IT SHALL LIE

KNOWLEDGE IS MODEST, CAUTIOUS AND PURE
IGNORANCE BOASTFUL, CONCEITED AND SURE

WHATEVER YOU ARE, BE THAT.
WHATEVER YOU SAY, BE TRUE.
STRAIGHTFORWARDLY ACT,
BE HONEST IN FACT
BE NOBODY ELSE BUT YOU

DO NOBLE THINGS, NOT DREAM THEM ALL DAY
   LONG
(Torquay pottery)

WORDS ARE EASY
LIKE THE WIND
FAITHFUL FRIENDS
ARE HARD TO FINE
1766

EDMUND FISHLEY MAKER FREMINGTON JUNE 6
   1839
WM. MILDON, HALSWELL, CHITTLEHAMPTON, 1839
THE TULIP AND THE BUTTERFLY
APPEAR IN GAYER COATS THAN I
LET ME BE DRESS'D FINE AS I WILL
FLIES, WORMS, AND FLOWERS EXCEED ME STILL

RICHD & MARY DINNIS MONKLEIGH MAY 12 1836
THE TULIP AND THE BUTTER FLY
APPEARS IN GAYER THINGS THAN I
LET ME BE DREST FINE AS (I WILL)
FLISE WORMS AND FLOURS EXCEED ME STILL

LONG MAY YOU LIVE
HAPPY MAY YOU BE
BLESS WITH CONTENT
AND FROM MISFORTUNES FREE

KIND WORDS ARE THE MUSIC OF THE WORLD
(Watcombe)

BE CAUSE I'M SMOL
FEL ME OFTEN HIL
PLES YOU ALL
EDMUND FISHLEY MAKER 1824

IF YOU'RE DOWN IN THE MOUTH,
THINK OF JONAH,
HE CAME UP ALRIGHT
(Watcombe)

A token from a friend

BUT I HAVE REMEMBERED YOU AND BOUGHT A
    TOKEN
FROM WINTERTHUR 1680

(Swiss faience)

1851/SARAH DAVIES/GLANDWR PARSH OF
    LANEGWAD/
GIVEN BY RACHAEL JONENES/MADE BY THOMAS
    ARTHUR/
EWENNY GLAMORGAN SHIRE/ SOUTH WALES
    NOVEMBER 20/1830

(on a globular money box)

THIS LITTLE JUG
IN FRIENDSHIP TAKE
AND KEEP IT FOR
THE GIVERS SAKE
REBECCA SEARLE
JUNE 6 1839

THE GEFT IS SMALL BUT GOOD WILL IS ALL   GM JG
    1792

(WHE)N THIS YOU SEE REMEMBER ME
AND KEEP ME IN YOUR MIND
LEET ALL MEN STILL SAY WHAT THEY WILL
SPEAK OF ME ASS YOU FIND
THEY ROSE IS READ THEY GRAS IS GREEN
THIS IS MY POT TILL I AM DEAD

THE ROSE IS RRED E LEAF IS GREEN YE DAYS ARE
    PAST THAT
WE HAVE SEEN 1791 IC BC SW

WHEN THIS YOU
SEE PRAY THINK ON
MEE AND BEAR IT IN
YOUR MIND FOR I AM SILL
TIMES AT YOUR HOUSE
SPEAK BY ME AS YOU FIND

EXCEPT THIS GEFT
MY DEAR FROM MEE

DESPISE ME NOT BECAUSE I'M SMALL
FILL ME OFTEN I'LL PLEASE YOU ALL

MADE BY JOHN SIGGERY POTTER WISTOW SUSSEX
FOR WILLIAM TERRY APSLEE THAKEHAM SUSSEX
    OCTR 7 1812

MISS ANN WILLIAMS
1866

PAUL MAY PLANT
AND APPOLOS WATER
BUT GOD GIVES
ME INCREASE
BIDEFORD
1866

1770 NO STAR SO BRIGHT AS MY DELIGHT

I LOVE BUT YOU ALONE   1738 MW 1738

Love and Marriage

ALL MAIDENS ON THE EARTH WOULD LIKE TO HAVE
    A MAN

(Odenwald, nr Spessart, 1719)

AS A RING IS ROUND
AND HATH NO END
SO IS MY LOVE
UNTO MY FRIEND

(North Devon)

1708
IT IS CUPID'S
DART WOUND
ED MY HEART

MY FREND IS HE THAT LOUE ME WELL
BUT HO HE IS I CANNOT TELL. I.M. 1770

(6 cups, conjoined)

THE BEST IS NOT TO GOOD FOR YOU 1695

(2-handled posset)

Slipware bowl from Hessen with the inscription, 'Love in the spring is for the maiden, Anno 1897'.

1695
E E
WHEN THIS U C
REMEMBER ME

BRISK BE TO THE MED YOU DESIER
AS HER LOVE YOU MA REQUIRE

RED LIKE THESE HEARTS
IS THE PAIN OF LOVE

(German)

YOUR OWN HOME WITH ITS PEACE
IS PART OF PARADISE

'Humour'

I AM LIKE THE BARE-FOOT MONKS
THEY ARE POOR AND I AM NOT RICH
(Odenwald, eighteenth century)

WIFE NOT SHOUTING
DOG NOT BARKING
CAT NOT MAKING MIAOU
DO NOT HAVE ANY USE
(Simenthal, Switzerland)

AND YOU CAN POOK
AND YOU CAN SHOVE
BUT A SUSSEX PIG
HE WUN'T BE DRUV

BREAK ME NOT I PRAY IN
YOUER HAST FOR I TO NON
WILL GIVE DES TAST
(seventeenth century Metropolitan
chamber pot)

USE ME WELL AND KEEP ME CLEAN
I'LL NOT SAY WHAT I HAVE SEEN
(nineteenth century chamber pot)

OUR MAID SERVANT LOOKS VERY WELL
SHE IS EATING THE MEAT AND GIVING US THE
BONES
(Heimberg, 1805)

IN THIS DISH ARE THREE FISH
IF YOU COOK THEM I WILL EAT THEM
(Hamburg, Germany)

A BAD WIFE IS A LOT OF TROUBLE
O DEAR LORD PRESERVE ME FROM THIS
(Simenthal, Switzerland)

On a punch bowl made at Chailey:

THOUGH WE AT CHAILEY ARE BUT MEAN
WE DO THE THINGS THATS NEAT & CLEAN
THO X FRANCIS X JERES WE VALUE NOT
WE WILL TRY TO MAKE A CHIMNEY POT

MY MYSTER FOUND ME JUST AND TREW
AND WHY NOT ME AS WELL AS YOU

The potter's name is inlaid round the pediment of the bowl broken up into double letters within circles:
M.A. D.E. B.Y. R.O. B.T. B.U. S.T. O.W. C.H. A.I. L.Y. S.O. T.H. C.O. M.N. O.N. S.O. T.E. R.Y. S.E. P.T. 17 91

National Spirit

On two-handled mugs:
GENERAL ELECTION / SOUTH GLAMORGAN / JULY
19TH 1895 /
WYNDHAM QUIN / MAJORITY / 825
And on the back: UNION IS STRENGTH

GENERAL ELECTION / CARDIFF / JULY 18TH 1895 /
J. M. MACLEAN / MAJORITY / 824
On the back: UNDER DROS BYTH (UNION FOR EVER)

On jugs:
GWNEWCH BOB / PETH YN GYMRAEG, and
OES Y BYD I'R IAITH GYMRAEG
(DO EVERYTHING IN WELSH / THE WELSH
    LANGUAGE FOR EVER)

On a wassail bowl:
FFIOL DDEUNAW DDOLENOG YR HEN GYMRY GYDA'R
    MARI LLWYD
('*Vessel of eighteen loops of the old welsh folk for
the mary llwyd*')
(Ewenny, Wales)

SUCCESS TO THE FARMER,
THE PLOUGH AND THE FLAIL,
MAY THE LANDLORD EVER FLOURISH,
AND THE TENANT NEVER FAIL.

GOOD LUCK TO THE HOOF AND THE HORN
GOOD LUCK TO THE FLOCK AND THE FLEECE
GOOD LUCK TO THE GROWERS OF CORN
MAY WE ALWAYS HAVE PLENTY AND PEACE

LONG LIFE AND / SUCCESS TO THE / FARMER / 1819

HE THAT BY THE PLOUGH WOULD THRIVE
HIMSELF MUST EITHER HOLD OR DRIVE
MARCH 3RD   R FISHLEY, JUG

G.R. 1741
GOD BLESS KING GEORGE AND ALL HIS MEN
AND SEND ADMERELL VERNON HOME A GAIN

SEND THEM VICTORIOUS,
HAPPY AND GLORIOUS
LONG TO REIGN OVER US
GOD SAVE THEM BOTH
(On articles commemorating the coronation of
King Edward VII and Queen Alexandra –
Aller Vale)

GOD BLESS YOU, TOMMY ATKINS,
HERE'S YOUR COUNTRY'S LOVE TO YOU
SOUTH AFRICA 1899–1900
(On articles commemorating the Boer War –
Aller Vale)

Your good Health

FILL UP THE GLASS SO THE GUEST WILL BE VERY HAPPY
AND WILL PRAISE YOU AND BE GRATEFUL
(Langnau, 1786)

A popular verse found on several different
examples of spirit flasks:

THIS LITTLE BOTTLE HOLDS A DROP
THAT WILL OUR DROOPING SPIRITS PROP
IT IS GINEVA CHOICE AND GOOD
TWILL CHEER THE HEART AND WARM THE BLOOD
(Sussex – inlay)

On a spirit flask made in 1812:

A LITTLE HEALTH
A LITTLE WEALTH
A LITTLE HOUSE TO LIVE IN:
AND AT THE END
A LITTLE FRIEND
AND A LITTLE CAUSE TO NEED HIM

And on the reverse of the same flask:

FOR SAMUEL WEEB
BRICK MAKER
WICK BRICK YARD
BRIGHTON SUSSEX
DECEMBER 2 1812

On another spirit flask:

ORCANS OF BRANDY
RIVERS OF WINE
FOUNTAINS OF TEA
& A GIRL TO MY MIND

And on the reverse:
GIVEN TO
EMMA GOLDSMITH
BATTLE, SUSSEX, 1835

FILL THIS CUP AND DRINK IT UP

GOOD DRINK MAKES EVERYONE YOUNG
(German)

On a punch bowl:

FILL YOUR GLASSES LAD AND LASSES
ROUND THE MAYPOLE FRISK AND PLAY
SMILING GLANCING SINGING DANCING
THIS IS CUPID'S HOLLIDAY

LET US DRINK & BE MERRY AND ENJOY OURSELVES
BUT NEVER TAKE TOO MUCH   MODERATION IS
    WELL IN ALL THINGS
(German)

THE APPLES OF DEVON MAKE CIDER SO FINE
TRY HUNTS DEVON CIDER, IT'S BETTER THAN WINE

Clay and the written word

DRINK ROUND MY JOVIAL
FELLOWS AND WHEN THAT
THIS IS DONE WE'LL HAVE
THE OTHER JUG MY BOYS
AND SING A MERY SONG
AUGUST 25 1818 WM OUGH QUATHIOCK

WINE CHEERS THE HEART
AND WARMS THE BLOOD
AND AT THIS SEASON'S MIGH
TY GOOD

THE POTTER FASHIONED ME COMPLETE,
AS PLAINLY DOTH APPEAR
FOR TO SUPPLY THE HARVEST MEN WITH
GOOD STRONG ENGLISH BEER
DRINK ROUND MY JOLLY REAPERS AND
WHEN THE CORN IS CUT WE'LL HAVE
THE OTHER JUG BOYS AND CRY
A NECK A NECK
      ABLE SYMONS   1813

WHEN YOU YOUR FRIENDS YOU DO INVITE THERE
    HEARTS AND FOR TO CHEAR
O THEN I PRAY MAKE USE OF ME AND FILL ME WITH
    STRONG BEER
AND WHEN THAT YOU TOGETHER SIT YOUR SELVES
    FOR TO DIVERT
THEN FILL YOUR CUP AND DRINK ABOUT A HEALTH
    WITH ALL YOUR HEART

KIND SIR : I COM TO GRATIFIEY YOURE KINDNESS
    LOVE AND
COURTISY AND SARVE YOURE TABLE WITH STRONG
    BEARE FOR THES
INTENT I WAS SENT HEARE ; OR IF YOU PLEAS I WILL
    SUPPLY YOUR WORKMEN WHEN IN
HARVEST DRY WHEN THEY DOE LABOUR HARD AND
    SWEATE GOOD DRINK IS BETTER FAR THEN MEAT

NOW I AM COME FOR TO SUPPLY YOUR WORKMEN
    WHEN IN
HARVIST DRY WHEN THEY DOE LABOUR HARDE AND
    SWEAT GOOD DRINK
IS BETTER FAR THAN MEATE : IN WINTER TIME
    WHEN IT IS COOLD I LIKEWISE
THEN GOOD DRINKE CAN HOULD : BOOTH SEASONS
    DOE THE SAME REQUIRE AND MOST
MEN DOE GOOD DRINKE DESIRE

LIVE LOVE AND LAUGH
                        (wine jug, German)

WHEN WAS IN MY NATIVE PLACE
I WAS A LUMPE OF CLAY
AND DIGGED UP OUT OF THE EARTH
AND BROUGHT FROM THENS A WAY
BUT NOW A JUG I AM BECOME
BY POTTERS ART AND SKILL
AND I YOUR SERVANT AM BECAME
AND CARIE ALE I WILL
      JOHN PHILLIPS
      1760

COME FILL ME
FULL AND DRINKE
A BOUT AND NEVER
LEAVE TILL ALL IS OUT
AND IF THAT WILL NOT
MAKE YOU MERRY
FILL ME AGAIN
AND SING DOWN
DERRY   1766

WORK ON BRAVE
BOYS AND NEVER FEAR
YOU SHALL HAVE ALE,
CYDER AND BEER, BEEF
PORK A_D PUDDING AS I
THINKE IS REAR GOOD
EATING WITH STRONG
      DRINKE
      1771

IN HARVEST TIME WHEN WORK IS HARD
INTO THE FIELD I MUST BE CARR : D
FULL OF GOOD CYDER OR STRONG BEER
YOUR THIRSY WORK FOLKS FOR TO CHEER
BUT IF YOU DO LEAVE ME AT HOME
BUT LITTLE WORK THERE WILL BE DONE
FOR WORK IS HARD AND DAYS ARE LONG
I HOPE YOUR LIQURE WILL BE STRONG

DRINK BE MERRY AND MARY
GOD BLES CREAE GEORGE & QUEEN ANN
JOHN MIER MADE THIS CUP 1708
                (3-handled pot holding two gallons)

COME GOOD WEMAN DRINK OF THE BEST
I HON MY LADY AND ALL THE REST

W
W E
THE RIT GENNRAL JORNAL
OFER THE DROUNK KEN
REGMENT NH 1618
(Wrotham, 'Fountain', Royal Arms, embossed)

FILL ME FULL DRINK OF ME WHILE YOU WOUL
    S O   1762
                          (fuddling cup)

DESPISE ME NOT
BECAUSE I'M MADE OF CLAY
BUT MAKE WE WELLCOME
WHEN I COME THIS WAY
MY BELLY FILL WITH GOOD STRONG
PUNCH OR BEER. AND I WILL
MAKE YOU MERRY ALL THE YEAR

THE GIFT OF RD. WHEELER 1798

ROBART POOL MAD THIS CUP
WITH A GUD POSSET FIL AND
                          (3-handled posset)

1670 JOHN WAYMAN JF
COME BROTHER SHAL WE IOYN GIVE ME
YOVE TWO
PENCE HERE IS IS MINE   (bellied jug)

COME FILL ME FULL WITH LIQUOR SWEET
FOR THAT IS GOOD WHEN FRIENDS DO MEET
BUT PRAY TAKE CARE DON'tT LET ME FALL
LEAST YOU LIST YOUR LIQUOR JUG AND ALL.
    CATHERINE DAVIES AGED 8 YEARS   (jug)

FILL ME FULL OF LIQUOR SWEET FOR THAT IS GOOD
    WHEN FRIENDS DO MEET.
WHEN FRIENDS DO MEET AND LIQUOR PLENTY. FILL
    ME AGAIN WHEN I.B.M.T.

FILL ME OF SIDFUL AND DRINK . . . RS. SP. VM.
    MAKER
THE GIFT IS SMALL. BUT GOOD WILL IS ALL. 1730
                          (6 cups, conjoined)

FILL ME FOR YOUR EASE
DRINK WHAT YOU PLEASE
1752. F.N.   (6 cups, conjoined)

WITH ALL MI HART I DRINK TO U
I WOLD HAVE BEERE BEFOR U GOO
    1705   A.B.O.B.
                          (Christening cup)

LO I UNTO YOUR HOUSE AM FENT
AS A TOKEN FROM A FRIND
WHEN YOUR HARVEST FOLKS ARE DRY
THEM I WILL THERE ATTEND. 1708
                          (large Harvest jug)

I DRINK TO YOU WITH ALL MU HART
MERY MET AND MERY PART. 1726.
                          (Christening cup)

Puzzle jug poems

FILL ME WITH ALE WITH WINE OR WATER
ANY OF THE 3 IT MAKES NO MATTER
DRINK ME DRY IF YOU ARE WILLING
IN DOING SO YOU'L WIN A SHILLING

WILLIAM COURTIC FEBRUARY 1 1791 JP

FROM ''MOTHER EARTH'' I CLAIM MY BIRTH
I'M MADE A JOKE FOR MAN
BUT NOW I'M HERE FILLED WITH GOOD CHEER
COME TASTE ME IF YOU CAN

HARRY D. BEANLAND / POLICE INSPECTOR /
    HALIFAX BORO'

GENTLEMEN NOW TRY YOUR SKILL,
ILL HOLD YOU SIXPENCE IF YOU WILL,
THAT YOU DON'T DRINK UNLESS YOU SPILL.

GENTLEMEN DRINK
_ LET YOUR SKILL BE TESTED
& A FORFEIT MADE
IF ANYTHING
BE WASTED

WITHIN THIS JUG THERE IS GOOD LIQUOR
'TIS FIT FOR PARSON OR FOR VICAR
BUT HOW TO DRINK AND NOT TO SPILL
WILL TAX THE UTMOST OF YOUR SKILL
(C. H. Brannam's Pottery, Barnstaple, North
                          Devon)

OS CEISIR OM CYNMWYSIAD (WRTH REOL)
ARFEROL RHIW DDRACHIAD
GOFALER PWY GYFEIRIAD
AI IR LLWNC, NEU ALLEN RHED
WILL O FON

*(If one seeks for my contents (as a rule), usually
some small draught, let him be careful in what
direction it goes to the gullet, or out it will flow)*

Lidded tobacco jar, with sgraffito inscription Andrew Crawford 1885, probably Buckley ware. 7″ high, and complete with interior clay stopper to keep the contents moist.

Miscellaneous

On a tobacco cannister:

MY TOBACCO I DO PUT
WITHIN THIS LITTLE POT
AND MY FRIEND MAY HAVE A PIPE
IF ANY I HAVE GOT

On a teapot, with a capacity of 7 pints:

MY LORDLY STATURE DO NOT FEAR
CHAMPIONS OF THE CHIT-CHAT BOARD
WHEN I AM FILLED FOR YOU THE FAIR
STREAMS OF COMFORT I'LL AFFORD
POUR IT OUT IN COPIOUS MEASURE
SIT AND DRINK AND TAKE YOUR PLEASURE

On a tobacco jar:

TOBACCO = HELP YERSEL

(Brewer – Longpark)

On a tobacco jar:

YOQ THAT ARE MY FRIEND ARE WELCOME TO MY
    INDIA WEED

A PIPE LETS TAKE
FOR OLD TIME'S SAKE

I AM BUT SMALL OR SUGER'S DEAR
OF IT BE SURE THAT YOU TAKE CARE
    MOLLEY SAVEALL 1791

(2-handled jar and cover)

IF YOU SOME SHUGER NOW HAVE GOT
PRAY PUT IT IN THIS LITTLE POT 1791

Praise the Lord

WITH THANKS I WILL PRAISE YOU MY GOD AND
    LORD HIGH
THERE IN HEAVEN. (THANKS BE TO GOD IN HIS
    HEAVEN)

(eighteenth century, Protestant plate)

O LORD SAVE ALL THOSE WHO GO TO SEA IN THIS
    SHIP

(Heinrich Segler, North Hamburg)

TRUST IN GOD WHO IS OUR HELP IN TROUBLE –
    MADE IN WINBERGEN
HOW WILL A YOUNG MAN MEND HIS WAYS
    WITHOUT SIN. ONLY IF HE LISTENS TO GOD'S
    WORD. ANNO 1838
I'LL BUILD BY HAPPINESS IN GOD AND NOT IN MY
    OWN MIND

(Protestant – large jug)

LITTLE BIRDS SING ON THE GREEN MEADOW

GOD SHALL BE PRAISED UNTO ALL ETERNITY
(Odenwald, 1779)

O MAN LOOK WHAT YOU DO REMEMBER YOU MUST
    DIE BUT GOD'S WORD
WILL STAY FOR EVER

(Glogau, Silesia, 1545)

German slip-trailed bowl with the inscription, 'With thanks will I praise you my good Lord in heaven on high'.

HEALTHY MIND, HEALTHY BODY
GOOD HEALTH AND GOOD NATURE
PLENTY OF MONEY AND GOD'S CARE WITH
    EVERYTHING
WHAT IS BETTER
(Langnau, dish)

IF YOU ARE HAVING A BAD TIME OR A GOOD TIME
    ALWAYS THANK GOD
(Langnau, porringer)

IF YOU HAVE SUFFICIENT TO EAT DON'T FORGET TO
    GIVE THANKS TO GOD.

BUCTON CASTLE CROSSING THE LINE
FROM ROCKS & SANDS AND EVERY ILL MAY GOD
    PROTECT THE SAILOR STILL
JOHN PHILIPS HOYLE 1857 BIDEFORD
SARAH NEWMAN 1860 JOHN HOYLE BIDEFORD
    1860
ELIZABETH COOP / OCEAN QUEEN / 1862
(Devon)

Clay, Earth and Death

AN EPITAPH
SHALL WE ALL DIE
WE SHALL DIE ALL
ALL DIE SHALL WE
DIE ALL WE SHALL

EARTH I AM, ET ES MOST TRU.
DESPISE ME NOT, FOR SO BE YOU.
(Aller Vale)

TODAY I
TOMORROW YOU
(To commemorate a dead child – Silesia,
sixteenth century)

Inscription on the tombstone prepared for
himself by John Weller :

IT IS FROM CLAY I MADE MYSELF
NOW I AM TURNED TO CLAY MYSELF

But his family disliked the inscription and
substituted instead :

HIS END WAS PEACE.
BEHOLD THE LAMB OF GOD WHICH TAKETH AWAY
THE SINS OF THE WORLD.

Designs for a bowl to commemorate
a birth – see page 34.

Part 3 Business affairs

10 Commissions, marketing, pricing

One-off commissions

It is a delicate business, establishing a firm order
with your customer, particularly if it is
something out of the ordinary. It is extremely
difficult to achieve a balance between the
hopelessly unattractive design he wants (for
example, a picture of the factory) and the kind
of design that can look well trailed or scratched
within the circular frame of a large wall-plate.
The whole performance is a kind of dance – one
step forward, two back – and unless he is paying
an extra design fee, you can do no more than
scribble ideas in his presence. In any event, the
difference between a neat drawing, done with a
pen, and the fluid result of slip-trailing is so
great that, in the end, it is not helpful.

The plates that I make to record weddings and
similar events in people's lives are not very
expensive – tens, not hundreds of pounds, so it
is a fairly simple matter to come to an agreement

with the customer at this level. When it comes
to work for industry it is a different matter, as
often companies want their logo as a central
motif, something unlikely to marry with
slipware techniques, and it is quite difficult to
persuade them to a more pictorial approach.

Sometimes an international company will
want a presentation plate for the director, fifty
ashtrays for the reps : and one hundred mugs for
office staff. In this instance there are certain
guidelines to be observed : having reached a
decision on your price, it is sensible to ask for
half the total sum agreed in advance, the balance
to be paid on delivery. This sort of contract
certainly concentrates the client's mind and
covers your initial costs. Knowing that you will
receive the balance of payment on completion of
the job also encourages you to complete the
order punctually. If you have a well-designed
label on the base of each pot, this can produce
some sort of feedback.

Customers may write and ask you to post them your design for, say, a small house plaque. Unfortunately, time spent in this operation will prove out of all proportion to the amount of cash received for the job. A written or verbal indication of what you hope to do, such as a simplified apple tree, is all that is needed. This leads me to mention that if you have the courage, do ask for a stamped addressed envelope. Postage at current rates means only about seven letters to the pound, and all this cost mounts up.

It seems that people often want their houses depicted on commemorative plates and they are seldom thatched cottages! Do ask for lots of photographs taken from all angles, *not* a drawing, and charge at least another £10 for the commission: you must always do this for any designs that are outside your own discipline.

In sgraffito work there are many design problems involved in placing square subjects in a circle, and latterly I have tackled this problem by firmly ruling a line near the bottom of the well of the plate and putting the wording within that space, as opposed to my usual practice of placing the inscription round the rim. This rim space can then be used to pick up some relevant theme in the brief.

Although I never trace designs, I always draw something as difficult as the client's house full-scale for my plate and cut out the paper outline. This template can be moved around on the surface area, along with trees, boats, dogs, etc., to make a coherent design, which you can then gently mark round with a pointed tool. This, of course, only applies to the sgraffito ware where the surface is leather-hard and not damaged by the paper. When it comes to slip-trail commissions, you can work from a sketch placed in front of you, preferably on a table music-stand. Because you are able to fill in your initial outline with other slips this enables you to cover over any small 'drawing' errors. If all else fails, the whole plate can be washed off and used again the next day. For a more expensive commission I always have two plates available so that if there is a disaster, the second one can be slipped in readiness for decoration. It must be remembered that life is greatly simplified by

decorating all work that is to be slip-trailed while the pot is still attached to the bat (see technical section, page 25).

For the simple daily work of marriage and anniversary plates, I have devised a small leaflet showing photographs of the basic designs (bride and groom, tree of life, house in bower, basket of flowers, etc.); and for the birth plates, rocking horse and Noah's Ark. On the reverse of the leaflet is a simple order form to fill in with an empty space for new prices and a clear indication that the customer must enclose a cheque with his order. Remember that you cannot ever re-sell such a plate. If you make a spelling mistake, the completed pot has to go in the dustbin.

Presenting and packaging your work is important if you service orders by post, but remember that the high cost of specially designed boxes has to be recovered by selling a lot of work.

Do not start a mail-order service unless you have a lot of capital and plenty of willing staff to process your mail, pack pottery *and* take these precious parcels to the post office. Otherwise your working day can be dangerously reduced.

Design based on the arms of Lincoln cathedral, for a bowl.

Fortunately I have been unable to design packaging for my large 12 inch diameter plates, and I hunt for supermarket boxes and waste packaging in skips. The rims of plates must be firmly protected by wads of newspaper, wood-wool or plastic foam. It is worth the small expense of a compensation form from the post office to insure more valuable parcels.

If the customer receives his plate intact and beautifully decorated but with a verbal inaccuracy – wrong date, ALAN spelt as ALLEN, for example – ask him to return it to you. You have to remake it and post it back. Naturally your charges will have allowed for these only too frequent disasters, and you must endeavour to keep a cheerful face in these difficult circumstances.

Remember that if the work is good to look at, nicely finished and arrives in one piece, on time, with a new order form, you may get the customer's or recipient's friends and family as future customers. A thoughtful public relations exercise is worth a certain amount of time and trouble, and possibly the best profit you make will come from this kind of order. One customer in three-hundred will write and thank you. I keep a very slim file of these letters, and treasure them.

Marketing

Craftsmen worry endlessly about inspiration and their fitness and competence as artists, when perhaps their energies would be better concentrated on marketing. It is a fact that has never ceased to astonish me in my many contacts with other potters and, indeed, on prestigious crafts committees, that professionalism and profit are still dirty words.

Before you decide to make your living as a potter, make sure you know where and how you are going to sell the pots. Unlikely as it may seem, there are very few authentic craft shops. There are many shops run by dilettantes who begin by buying only home-produced crafts, but soon buy in from Third World countries. Whatever the moral arguments, the difference in price between mass-produced, low labour-costed Indian artefacts and work made by local designer-craftsmen is so extreme that it seriously damages the local potter's market.

There are, of course, art galleries which sell non-functional sculptural ceramics that are in sympathy with the prints they display on their walls. This type of gallery is excellent for the more 'abstract' ceramist, but quite hopeless for slipware potters: we are still seen as copyists of Thomas Toft and, at worst, as purveyors of folk art souvenirs.

There is a third type of gallery run lovingly by its owners who take a real interest in their craftsmen and display the work well, but you will find that even they, after a couple of years, are looking for something different to stimulate their customers' interest. They want to ring the changes, and it will take a lot of work on the craftsman's part in telephone calls, visits and presenting new lines to make it possible for his pots to stay in the same gallery over several years.

It is necessary by extensive research to find a gap in the market, whether it be for decorated tiles or garden pots. You will discover there is little demand for an ill-thought-out container jar that does not hold either a half or one kilo

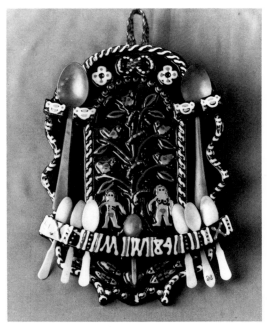

Spoon rack with slip trailing and applied decoration. 14″ high.

capacity and is not related to similarly decorated wares.

Nevertheless, if your work is truly individual, lively and different, you will find an outlet for it, even if you begin, as I did, by selling at county shows and craft fairs. This exposes you to the public and you must learn and respond to the customers' comments on your work. The reaction will be different in different parts of the country.

After this primary marketing exercise, when you have managed to produce a consistent range of pots out of your kiln, you still have to arrive at two price ranges: the retail and the wholesale (ideally the latter should be only 10 per cent less than your retail price). The next problem is how to deliver work to a distant shop. Do you take a day off work to deliver it? How can you cost this into the pots? Who is in the workshop to answer the telephone and see potential customers? If the shop is a three-hour journey away, how are you going to rationalize the wear and tear on your old van as well as the cost of the petrol? Few shop owners are prepared to come and collect the work, but if they do it is worth offering them lunch and a glass of wine. Time spent in this way consolidates good relations and makes them want to come again, and it is much cheaper than your journey to them.

If you send the work by a road carrier, remember that a full tea-chest costs about as much as a new jacket, and a whole day must be spent in packing satisfactorily and listing the contents. You cannot insure breakables with many carriers. If the gallery pays for this expense then it has to go on to the price of the pot, plus the gallery's 100 per cent mark-up, and this makes the work so expensive that no-one will buy it. There are no easy answers to this problem. You will have to search for your individual solution, but do remember that time is money!

In order to keep the books straight, it is essential to present yourself professionally, and this means investing in some well designed stationery and some nicely produced graphics. A clear and well thought-out card incorporating your address and telephone number is vital, and

Bowl, 12″ diameter, with a motif derived from the sketches on the previous page.

work is also very useful. Once the original art-work has been completed, it is not expensive to have one hundred or so copies printed in black and white. Try to find the money to commission a special label, as opposed to the very cheap, self-adhesive ones used by everyone else. People will learn to recognize your image, not just from the objects themselves but from your presentation.

Instead of using newspaper and old supermarket bags, it is better to invest in a ream of tissue paper, some plain paper bags and plastic carriers, none of which is very expensive. A group of craftsmen can buy these things in bulk which cuts the costs even further.

You must accept that at least 45 per cent of your time will be taken up with boring administration, instead of the exciting and creative work on the wheel. Somewhere in these demanding days you must find time to visit your own capital city, see the shops and markets, find out what people are wearing and buying, get a feel for the contemporary trend. You do not have to pursue trendiness at all costs, but can respond to your instincts, at the same time as being aware of the fashion.

some distinctive motif (if necessary, a map) and perhaps your opening hours or 'by appointment' will help. A leaflet with a picture of the craftsman at the wheel, a few words on your sources of inspiration and training, and preferably some photographic detail of your

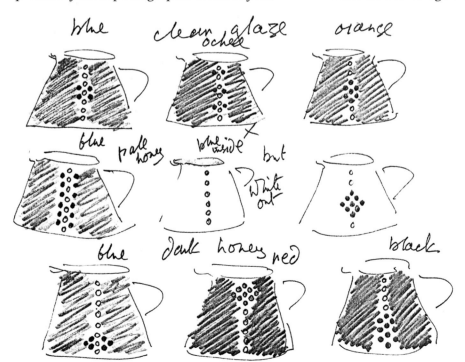

Alternative decoration schemes for a small cream jug, based on a Swiss design. Not only can the engobe colour be varied, but likewise the colours of the dots.

124

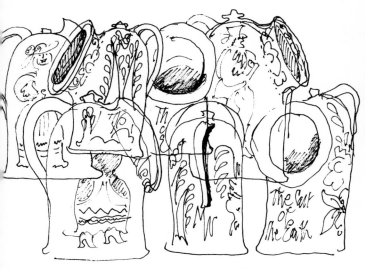

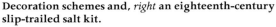

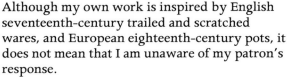

Decoration schemes and, *right* **an eighteenth-century slip-trailed salt kit.**

Although my own work is inspired by English seventeenth-century trailed and scratched wares, and European eighteenth-century pots, it does not mean that I am unaware of my patron's response.

Every form has its history: the egg stand shown on page 68, first seen in the Fitzwilliam Museum in Cambridge, suddenly becomes a window into its seventeenth-century past – boiled eggs with a receptacle for salt. There is no reference in early cookery books to an egg eaten from its shell. So, was this great pot made for Gargantua? Did he sit down to six eggs and throw the shells on the table to be collected by the serving man? And how was the salt kept dry before it came here? Of course, in the salt kit with its dome and open mouth. If you did not live near the sea or an inland salt mine, the purveyor may only have come four times in the year with a supply to preserve your meat and savour your vegetables. How precious these grains must have been. From the large archetype, 7 inches high, I developed a small

salt kit $3\frac{1}{2}$ inches high, partly for my own pleasure but also for tourists from abroad to pack in their hand-luggage as they return home – an authentic English folk pot, but small and light enough to travel comfortably. I make these pots, with both their past and their present-day efficiency in mind. I make a half-pint jug, enriched with its West Country doggerel or Yeatsian poem, but made with a broad base so it does not tip over on the breakfast tray.

The Owl jug, with its lidded cup that served a ritual function, was principally an ornament and was used once or twice a year as a loving cup. The form was prevalent in Germany in the eighteenth century in tin glaze, but back in the thirteenth century it was presented as an archery prize, and made of bronze. I have always been fascinated with the typical seventeenth- and eighteenth-century Staffordshire owl jugs, the earlier ones rather simple and sturdy in execution, while the later ones are delicate on their small pedestals with applied wings and tail. Their whole being is

125

coffee pot   1794

5*

owl

anno
1794

Commissions, marketing, pricing

covered in a complex marbled and feathered slip, extraordinarily difficult to execute as it must be worked on all over while it is wet enough to disturb the surface with both movement and feather (see page 28).

Amongst the potter's customers can be found pig collectors and cat collectors, as well as owl afficionados. I have not yet made an elephant or a mouse, but there are collectors of those as well.

In the Haslemere museum in Surrey there is a collection of folk art which I have studied at length. From a working day there emerged a project to produce a small 'German' coffee bowl with two looped handles. It proved difficult to make and time consuming to apply the looped handles: decorating inside the deep bowl seemed tremendously clumsy with the slip trailer, but slowly a satisfactory form emerged and in time a small black bowl hangs on the dresser, its decoration held together with precisely placed dots. Then, miracle of miracles, a customer comes in and asks 'How much is it?' The project becomes successful and I continue to make the bowls, finding better ways to attach the handles, simpler forms of decoration, new colours and new variations, but all inspired by that small, stag-decorated wood-fired nineteenth century *Kafee Schüssel* in the museum.

Ideas and projects for new lines are always buzzing round in the potter's head, and they can slowly be shaped in the workshop until you are ready tentatively to expose them in trade or craft fairs, or in your own showroom area. If the response is minimal and practically no-one buys, they must be abandoned. On the other hand, sometimes a customer's request for a special kind of pot will initiate a satisfactory new line which will sell.

The initial investment in attending a trade fair may seem far from trivial, but buyers come from far and wide, from department stores, mail-order catalogues and small shops. There is also the opportunity to see other craftsmen's offerings, and on talking to them you will learn from their experiences. You will find that one or two firm orders will cover your initial costs, and if you follow up the many tentative enquiries three or four weeks later this will help to consolidate further orders.

A deep hanging bowl with a design inspired by the eighteenth-century *Kafee Schüssel* drawn on the facing page.

It is not advisable to take a wholesale order for under £100 ($150). The more of your pots that a shop owner has, the more he is encouraged to make a good display of your work, not just to scatter one or two items among the other stock. Your leaflet will be of help here, as he may reproduce some information from it to display, perhaps with your photograph alongside the work. Thus the pots are no longer nameless and the customer will be encouraged to return and ask for more.

Pricing

Pricing work is an area of major difficulty for the aspiring craftsman, and one that is not easily resolved. The spectre of an extra 100 to 120 per cent on your selling price that many shops will place on your work seems to numb the mind, but do not forget that not everyone is as poor as you are. Some people shopping at Liberty's, for instance, will expect to pay £75 (or more than $100) for a small, well designed, satisfying, hand-made object knowing that it is unique.

Underpricing your work will only strike a blow at other struggling craftsmen whose work will be seen as too expensive. Somehow you have to cover your costs, otherwise the confrontation with your bank manager about your overdraft will become increasingly acrimonious. Fortunately, as the old Devon, German, French, Italian and Spanish potters say, 'This pot is made of earth and when it breaks the potter laughs'.

When I started my small pottery in 1974 it was possible to buy all the equipment needed, pay the bills and start to earn a small income from the pots, for a capital outlay of £2,000 ($3,000). Now, in 1985, it is difficult to buy one medium-sized kiln for under £800 ($1200), and a good electric wheel costs £500 ($750). The labour costs for installing a kiln are phenomenal, and soon your electricity consumption will be the most expensive item on your budget as you will probably have a minimum of one bisque and one glost firing per week. A commemorative potter has to have a short work cycle so as to be able to deliver the commission about three weeks after taking the order.

Pricing has to be very flexible. There is the price from your own workshop which should allow for a small profit on costs and time. When your work goes away to a gallery for an exhibition you have to find out what their exact mark-up will be. Often this is $33\frac{1}{3}$ per cent, plus VAT, which generally means you have to add 50 per cent on to your retail price, to estimate the price at which the goods will be selling in the gallery. The owner will need a list of all your pots, with prices, and you must make sure that you indicate clearly whether the price is your price or the gallery selling price. If you cannot type, make a photocopy of your handwritten list, as this is invaluable reference material.

A shop buying your work will need a wholesale price and, as stated before, they will usually be putting a 100 per cent mark-up on the pots. Your wholesale price should be approximately 10 per cent less than your retail price. It is advisable to have a wholesale price list, nicely designed with your logo at the top and preferably simple line drawings of your work. Order only one hundred copies from the original art-work. When your ideas and prices change it is quite easy to block out the old

drawings and prices with a sticky label, re-write them and have them photocopied again.

There is no way that you can price your time for every item that you make. Some things reflect little profit and they are offset by the pieces where you are able to allow for a good profit margin. As a simple guide, your customer will not expect to pay much for domestic functional ware, such as a cereal bowl, butter dish, mug, supper plate, etc., but he will be prepared to pay a good deal more for an important gift, such as a large decorated cheese platter, a large fruit bowl or an important ornamental jug. These pieces will make you some profit, and these are also the pots that are exciting to make, but greedy of space in the kiln and expensive as a speculative venture.

The moment that you put lids on pots, or handles, or additional knobs and feet, eyes and legs, it increases the time you spend and can make the exercise uneconomic. I make a small owl jug where I press in the sockets and apply a small pad to represent the eye. Both the pot and the eye-ball have to be keyed and 'slushed' and the whole area carefully cleaned to prevent any roughness appearing under the glaze. This apparently simple operation takes longer (and is also more boring) than inscribing a short poem on the front of a half-pint jug, and it therefore has to be priced accordingly.

When you have designed something new to add to your range, price it 'sensibly': if it sells well you can slowly increase the price. If people do not show much interest initially, keep the price low for six months and if it still does not sell, abandon it.

If the price cannot reflect the time taken on the pot, it *must* cover the cost of your rent, rates, fuel bills, petrol, car maintenance, etc., as well as simple living. When I started my business, the only way I could find to price the work was to make each kiln load represent £150 ($225), but the price must depend on the size of the kiln.

Unfortunately the market-place is full of work made by 'hobby' potters who are financed by their spouse and work at home. Their costing is geared to supporting their hobby, i.e. paying for clay and glaze materials, and petrol. Your work has to sell at double this amount, but remember you are aiming for higher things. To keep afloat you must remember to include mortgage, bank interest on overdraft, wages, building maintenance, kiln and wheel maintenance, kiln furniture replacements, clay, glaze material, stationery, photography, graphics – the list goes on and on. You can, therefore, see that a tea pot selling in a craft shop for £6.50 is made either by an amateur or an idiot – make sure you are not one of these.

Despite all the very relevant financial considerations and the stringent disciplines of the medium itself, the life of the slipware potter is full of interest and pleasure. In a society where the machine threatens to take over the role of man, leaving him often without dignified occupation, the role of the slipware potter is unusually effective: for he, in a sense, makes reality of his clients' dreams, providing the link between the earth and the making, as well as unashamedly conveying sentiment. Writing on the pot the message 'from Ron to Mary with love. May 1986' can be a poignant message, a piece of family history. The skill is traditional but concern with the past does not conflict with the realities of the present.

''We are always inside history.''

Glossary

With acknowledgments to Bernard Leach, *A Potter's Book*.

AGATE WARE is made of different coloured clays, left unmixed, in strata.

ALUMINA (CHINA CLAY or KAOLIN) withstands high temperatures, causes opacity in glazes and diminishes fusibility. An essential component of porcelain bodies, firing white. In most bodies 10–40 per cent of china clay is present.

ANTIMONY OXIDE with lead makes a yellow at low and medium temperatures. With iron oxide a wider colour range can be obtained. With other fluxes it behaves in the manner of tin oxide. Toxic.

BALL CLAY is a plastic clay, principally used to slip, which fires white or whitish and withstands a high temperature.

BARBOTINE is a term used to describe trailed decoration in high relief, usually done on dry body or biscuited ware.

BOCAJ A Hungarian milk jug.

BATS are wooden discs, placed on the wheel-head, on which the pots are thrown.

BISQUE/BISCUIT Unglazed fired ware.

BODY The clay of which a pot is made.

CALIPERS Sculptor's measuring tools, very useful for checking the diameters of pots, especially when throwing lids or covers.

CHINA CLAY *see* alumina.

COMBING is a method of decorating the wet surface of a pot with a blunt-toothed comb made of wood, leather or rubber.

CONES Orton and standard cones for gauging heat in kilns are made out of the constituents of glazes in the form of tall pyramids, and bend and melt at given temperatures, to indicate heat work.

C.O.S.I.R.A. Council of Small Industries in Rural Areas

C.P.A Craftsman Potters Association

CRAZING A faulty and unintentional crackling of a glaze.

DELFTWARE *see* Faience, majolica.

EARTHENWARE low-fired glazed wares with a permeable body.

ENGOBE Another word for slip, used throughout this text to describe a *pouring* slip.

FAIENCE Tin-glazed ware. *See also* majolica.

FETTLE To finish or smooth the surface of leather-hard clay.

FIRECLAYS are distinguished from pure clays on the one hand by a somewhat higher percentage of fluxes, and from siliceous refractory clays on the other by a lower percentage of free silica. They are usually found in nature below coal seams. They withstand high temperatures and are yellow or grey in colour.

FLATWARE Dishes, plates, saucers, bowls, etc., are known in the potteries by this name to distinguish them from hollow ware – jugs, mugs, etc.

GALENA Lead sulphide. A finely ground lead ore used from early time for glazing red and brown earthenwares. Not used today because of its toxicity.

GLOST FIRING The glaze firing.

GROG Powdered fired clay, ground to varying degrees of fineness and usually made from old pots.

HOLLOW WARE in distinction from flat ware is a trade name for those pots which are narrower at the mouth than at their main convexity.

JEWELLING A method of enhancing slip-trailed outline with small dots of contrasting colour. *See* pearling.

KAOLIN *see* alumina.

LEAD, as Galena or lead ore (usually an impure lead sulphide), red lead (litharge), or massicot (lead monoxide) and white lead (basic carbonate), has in all these forms been excessively employed as a fluxing agent for low and medium temperature glazes from early times. Toxic.

MAJOLICA The name given to tin-glazed pottery fired at earthenware temperatures, being a corruption of the name of the island of Majorca.

MEZZA-MAJOLICA A term formerly used to describe scratching and oxide painting done on the leather-hard earthenware body before firing and under a clear lead glaze.

OXIDATION The firing of a kiln in such a manner that combustion is complete and in consequence the burning gases are amply supplied with oxygen which causes metals in clay and glaze to give their oxide colours.

PATE-SUR-PATE A method of decoration developed in France which consists of building up a low relief on a clay body by repeated touches with a brush loaded with slip.

PEARLING A method of enhancing back slip-trailed outline drawing with small dots of slip.

PIPE CLAY The clays of which tobacco pipes were made, consisting of pure clays, marls or fireclays containing little or no iron.

PUG MILL A cylinder contracted at one end, containing revolving blades which compress, cut and mix plastic clays to produce a coherent body.

PYROMETERS Instruments for measuring the temperature within kilns. There are several types.

RAW GLAZING Once-firing, with the glaze applied to green ware.

REDUCTION in contradistinction to oxidation is a condition of burning gases in a kiln in which combustion is incomplete or smoky, the carbon present having the effect of reducing the oxides to their respective metal forms.

ROSEMALING The traditional rose decoration as on canal long-boats.

SADDLES or SHOULDERS Clay props used between plates when packed on edge in a kiln. Refractory bars of triangular cross section, saddles are alternatives to stilts.

SAGGARS Fireclay boxes in which pots are packed in a kiln to protect them from the direct action of the flames.

SCANDY A type of brushed and trailed slip design used by South Devon potters in the late nineteenth and early twentieth century.

SCUM Efflorescence or sulphation is caused before, during or after firing by soluble salts contained in the body. These can be neutralized by barium carbonate. At high temperatures such salts may combine with silica in the body and form a thin skin of glaze, e.g. salt glaze. In lower-temperature wares moisture may bring out a fresh efflorescence after firing. Any sulphur in the fuel (e.g. coal) or glaze (e.g. galena) is liable to form sulphuric acid and to combine with such salts, forming sulphates which appear as white or yellowish spots on the surface of the glaze.

S.D.C. Society of Designer Craftsmen

SGRAFFITO The decoration of leather-hard pots by scratching through an engobe to expose the colour of the clay or another engobe below.

SHARDS/SHERDS Broken pieces of pot, usually ancient and found on an archaeological site.

SHOULDERS *see* SADDLES.

SHRINKAGE During the process of drying and firing, clays vary in their contraction up to a maximum of about 25 per cent.

SLURRY A rough mixture of clay and water.

SOAKING Maintaining a temperature in a kiln firing, during which heat penetrates through the wares but does not rise as a whole. It usually lasts only $1-1\frac{1}{2}$ hours.

SPONGING Method of slip or oxide decoration using a small sponge.

SPRIGGING Method of applying decoration, using clay from small bisque or plaster moulds.

STILTS Clay tripod supports for firing glazed wares.

STONEWARE Pottery fired to a temperature (usually over 1200°C) at which the body vitrifies.

TERRACOTTA Low-fired unglazed red ware including much primitive pottery.

TRAILING A method of decorating semi-dry pots with thick slip, usually squeezed out of a rubber tube with a plastic or quill pipette.

TURNING Shaving and paring leather-hard clay from the walls or feet of pots on a lathe or potter's wheel.

WARPING of pots both whilst drying and in the kiln takes place from approximately the same cause: unequal heating and consequent uneven shrinkage.

WEATHERING The exposure of unrefined clay to the action of the elements over time, which improves the quality of the clay.

WEDGING A method of cutting, beating and reversing a mass of clay to expel air and make the whole homogeneous.

Bibliography

Artia and Tatran, *Slovak Folk Art*, London 1954

Artigas, Jose Llorens, *Spanish Folk Ceramics*, Barcelona 1970.

Ayres, James, *British Folk Art*, London 1977

Baines, John Manwaring, *Sussex Pottery*, Brighton 1980

Barber, Edwin A., *Tulip Ware of Pennsylvania*, New York 1970

Barton, K. J., *Buckley Pottery*, Buckley 1975

———, *Pottery in England from 3500 BC – AD 1750*, Newton Abbot 1975

Billington, Dora, *The Technique of Pottery*, London 1962

Bivins, John Jr., *The Moravian Potter in North Carolina*, North Carolina 1972

Bossert, H. Th., *Peasant Art in Europe*, Berlin 1938

Bradley, 'Story of Castle Hedingham Pottery.' *The Connoisseur*, Feb, March, April 1968

Brannam, Peter, *A Family Business*, Exeter 1982

Brears, Peter, *Collector's Book of English Country Pottery*, Newton Abbot 1974

———, *English Country Pottery housed in York Museum*, York 1968

———, *The English Country Pottery, its history and techniques*, Newton Abbot 1973

Burlington Fine Arts Club, *Exhibition of early English Earthenware*, London 1914

Burton, William, *English Earthenware and Stoneware*, London 1904

Caiger-Smith, Alan, *Tin-Glaze Pottery*, London 1973

Cashmore, C. & C., *Collard, the Honiton and Dorset Potter*, Essex 1983

Chaffers, William, *Marks and Monograms on Pottery and Porcelain*, London 1932

Charbonnier, T., *Notes on North Devon Pottery*, Devon Association 1906

Church, Arthur, *English Earthenware*, London 1894

———, *Catalogue of Old English Pottery*, London 1870

Clark, Kenneth, *Pottery and Ceramics*, London 1956.

Clay, 'Edward Bingham, Potter of Castle Hedingham', *The Connoisseur*, August 1934.

Cooper, Ronald, *English Slipware Dishes 1650–1850*, London 1968

———, *The Modern Potter*, London 1947

———, *The Pottery of Thomas Toft*, Catalogue of Exhibition at Leeds and Birmingham 1952

Crofts, J., *Packhorse, Wagon and Post Land Carriage and Communications under the Tudors and Stuarts*, 1967

Cuisenier, Jean, *Potiers de Saintonge – huit siècles d'artisanat rural*, Paris 1975

Davey, Peter, *Buckley Pottery*, Chester 1975

Domanovsky, György, *Hungarian Pottery*, Budapest 1968

———, *Kántor Sándor*, Budapest 1977

Downman, Edward A., *English Pottery and Porcelain*, London 1896

Draper, Jo, *Dated Post-Medieval Pottery in Northampton Museum*, Northampton 1975

Earle, Maj. Cyril, *Earle Collection of early Staffordshire Pottery*, London 1915

Evans, George Ewart, *From Mouths of Men*, London 1976

Fagone, *Artigianato Siciliano*, Rome 1966

Fay, Antoinette, *La Poterie Vernissée à Décor Gravé sur Engobe au seizième siècle*, Sèvres 1973

Fishley Holland, W., 'Fifty Years a Potter', *Pottery Quarterly*, Tring 1958

Fleming, J. A., *Scottish Pottery*, Glasgow 1923

Fry, Roger, *Vision and Design*, London 1937

Godden, Geoffrey, *British Pottery*, London 1976

Grant, Alison, *North Devon Pottery, the Seventeenth Century*, Exeter 1983

Gruffyd, K. Lloyd, *Seventeenth Century Bestiary ware from Buckley*, Clwyd

Guilland, Harold F., *Early American Folk Pottery*, New York 1971

Haggar, Reginald C., *English Country Pottery*, London 1950

Hartley, Dorothy, *Made in England*, London 1939

———, *Food in England*, London 1954

Hartley, Marie, & Joan Ingilby, *Life and Tradition in the Yorkshire Dales*, London 1968

Hasalova & Vajdis, *The Folk Art of Czechoslovakia*, Feltham 1974

Hobson, R. L., *Catalogue of English Pottery in the British Museum*, London 1903

Hodgkin, J. E. & E., *Examples of Early English Pottery, Named, Dated and Inscribed*, London 1891

Hofer & Fél, *Hungarian Folk Art*, Budapest 1975

Hole, Christina, *English Home-Life 1500–1800*, London 1947

Honey, W. B., *The Art of the Potter*, London 1946

———, *English Pottery and Porcelain*, London 1947

———, *European Ceramic Art*, London 1952

Istvan, Erzsébet, *Volkstümlice Keramik aus Ungarn*, Catalogue Düsseldorf Museum 1985

James, Susan, 'Barum Ware, The Work of C. H. Brannam', *Antique Collector* 1973

Jedding, Herman, *Volkstümliche Keramik*, Hamburg 1976

Jewitt, Llewellyn, *Ceramic Art of Great Britain*, 2 Vols, London 1878

Jones, Barbara, *The Unsophisticated Arts*, London 1951

Kemp, Dorothy, *English Slipware – How to Make It*, London 1954

Kresz, Maria, *Magyar népi cserépedények*, Budapest 1983

———, *Mezötúr Fazekassága 1813–1914*, Budapest 1978

———, *The Pottery of Csákvár*, Budapest 1976

Kuczyńska, Teresa, *Souvenir of Poland*, Warsaw 1978

Lambert, M. & Marx, Enid, *English Popular Art*, London & New York 1951

Lane, Arthur, *Style in Pottery*, Oxford 1948

Leach, Bernard, *Art of the Potter*, London 1940

———, *The Potter's Challenge*, Ed. David Outerbridge, London 1976

Leicester Museum – *Catalogue of the Permanent Collection*

of English Ceramics, Leicester 1953

Lewis, Griselda, *A Collector's History of English Pottery*, London 1969

———, *An Introduction to English Pottery*, London 1950

———, *A Picture History of English Pottery*, London 1956

Lipman, Jean and Alice Winchester, *The Flowering of American Folk Art 1776–1876*, New York 1974

Llubiá, Luis M., *Cerámica Medieval Española*, Barcelona 1968

Lomax, Charles, *Quaint Old English Pottery*, Manchester 1909

Matthews, Leslie, *Antiques of the Pharmacy*, London 1971

Meteyard, Eliza, *Life of Josiah Wedgwood*, 2 Vols., London 1865–7

Mountford, *Reports Nos. 3, 4, & 7, Archaeological Society, City of Stoke on Trent Museum*

Mountford and Celoria, *Some Examples of Sources in the History of Seventeenth Century Ceramics*, Stafford 1968

Nonell, Carmen, *Cerámica y Alfareria Populares de España*, Barcelona, 1973

Parkinson, Michael R., *The Incomparable Art*, Thomas Greg Collection, Manchester 1969

Pericot, Luis, *Céramique Ibérique*, Paris 1980

Pitkin, Alber Hastings, *Early American Folk Pottery*, Hartford, Conn. 1918

Plot, Robert, *The Natural History of Staffordshire*, Oxford 1685

Plymouth Museum, *Castle Street, The Pottery*, Archaeological Series No. 1, Plymouth 1979

Pollex, John, *Slipware*, London 1979

Powell, *Pennsylvania Pottery, tools and processes*, Pennsylvania 1972

Rackham, Bernard, *Catalogue of the Glaisher Collection, Fitzwilliam Museum*, 2 vols., Cambridge 1935

———, *Early Staffordshire Pottery*, London 1951

———, *Italian Majolica*, New York

———, & Read, H. *English Pottery: its development from early times to the end of the eighteenth century*, London 1924

Rada, P., *A Book of Ceramics*, London 1964

Read, Herbert, *Art and Industry*, London 1934

Rhead, G. W. & F. E., *Staffordshire Pots and Potters*, London 1906

Scholten-Neess, Mechthild, *Niederrheinische Bauerntöpferei 17th–19th Century*, Düsseldorf 1971

Shaw, Simeon, *History of the Staffordshire Potteries*, Hanley 1829

Solon, L. M., *The Art of the Old English Potter*, London 1883

Stradling, Diana & J. Garrison, (Eds.) *The Art of the Potter*, New York 1974

Sturt, George, *A Small Boy in the Sixties*, Sussex 1977

Taggart, Ross E., *Burnap Collection of English Pottery in William Rockhill Nelson Gallery, Atkins Museum*, Kansas 1967

Tait, Hugh, *Samuel Malkin – slipware dishes; Birds in European Ceramic Art, Part I – The Owl*, Apollo 1958.

Tyler, Sheila, *Buckley Pottery*, Exhibition at Mostyn Art Gallery, Llandudno 1983

Vydra, Josef and Ludvik Kunz, *Painting on Folk Ceramics (Slovakia)*, London 1949

Warsaw National Museum, *Folk Arts: Guide to the Permanent Exhibition, National Museum of Ethnography*, Warsaw 1981

Watkins, C. Malcolm, *North Devon Pottery, its Export to America in the Seventeenth Century*, Washington 1960

Watkins, Lura Woodside, *Early New English Potters and their Wares*, Cambridge, Mass., 1950

———, *Early New England Pottery, Old Stourbridge Village*, Cambridge, Mass., 1959

Weatherill, Lorna, *The Pottery Trade in North Staffordshire 1660–1760*, Manchester 1970

Webster, D. B., *Early Slip-Decorated Pottery in Canada*, Toronto 1969

Wills, Geoffrey, *English Pottery and Porcelain*, London 1969

———, 'English Pottery in 1969 – an unpublished document', *Apollo*, Vol. 64, June 1967

Wyss, Robert L., *Berner Bauernkeramik*, Bern, 1966

Picture credits

Alphabet & Image 1, 3, 14 (left), 17 (all), 18 (all), 20, 21 (all), 22 (left), 23 (all), 24, 25, (left – both, and bottom right), 26 (left), 27 (top right), 29 (right), 30 (all), 31, 36 (both), 37 (all), 60, 61 (bottom), 108, 118 (top), 119, 124, 127; American Museum, Bath 59; Claire Bogino 97; British Museum, London 28 (right); Burrell Collection, Glasgow 8; Christie, Manson and Woods 74; City Museum, Stoke-on-Trent 46; Colchester Museum 73; Ronald Cooper 44 (left); Marianne de Trey 76; Exeter Museum 56, 61 (top); Fitzwilliam Museum, Cambridge 34 (bottom), 43, 65, 67, 69, 70, 77, 80 (right), 85 (bottom), 89, 103 (bottom), 109 (left); Alan Frewin 75 (right); Grosvenor Museum, Chester 45; Hastings Museum 26 (right), 109 (right); Historiches Museum, Bern 85 (bottom); Landesmuseum, Trier 44 (right); Manchester City Art Gallery 11, 47 (top right), 47 (bottom right), 48, 49 (both), 62; Musée Carnavalet Beauvaisis 95 (top); Museum fur Kunste und Gewerbe, Hamburg 103 (top); Museum of London 29 (top), 39, 40, 134; National Ethnographical Museum, Budapest 98 (both), 99; National Ethnographical Museum, Warsaw 101 (all); National Trust 12; Phillip Oates Collection 53; Steffi Peltner 81; John Pollex 28 (left); La Revue de la Céramique 104; Francisco Catala Roca 86; Rouen Museum 58; Dr Scholten-Neess 78, Sèvres Museum 94, 95 (bottom); Jason Shackleton 75 (left); Shoot Photographics 4–5, 9, 13 (both), 14 (right), 15, 26 (bottom left), 27 (left and bottom), 29 (bottom left), 33, 34 (top left and right), 55 (top), 68 (bottom), 72, 84 (right), 96, 121, 125, 129; Jonathan Snell 41; John Solly 22 (right); Sothebys 52; Dr Spielmann 92; Victoria & Albert Museum, London 80 (left); Wallace Collection 57, 90; Welsh Folk Museum, St Fagan's 64; Mary Wondrausch 6, 25 (top right), 32, 47 (left), 51, 54, 55 (bottom), 68 (top), 88, 100, 106, 113, 114.

Museums
with important slipware collections

United Kingdom
CAMBRIDGE Fitzwilliam Museum
CARDIFF Welsh Folk Museum, St Fagans
CHESTER Grosvenor Museum
EDINBURGH Huntley House
EDINBURGH Royal Scottish Museum
GLASGOW William Burrell Collection
LEEDS City Art Gallery
LIVERPOOL City Museum
LONDON British Museum
LONDON Museum of London
LONDON Victoria & Albert Museum
MANCHESTER Whitworth Art Gallery
OXFORD Ashmolean Museum
SHEFFIELD Sheffield City Museum
STOKE-ON-TRENT Museum and Art Gallery
WADDESDON Waddesdon Manor, James A. Rothschild
Bequest
YORK York City Museum

United States of America
KANSAS CITY Nelson Gallery, Atkins Museum,
Burnap Collection
NEW YORK Metropolitan Museum
PHILADELPHIA Pennsylvania Museum

Switzerland
BERNE Musée de l'Histoire de Berne
BURGDORF Schloss Burgdorf
LANGNAU Heimat Museum
THUN Castle Museum
ZURICH Kunstgewerbemuseum
ZURICH Swiss National Museum

A seventeenth-century Staffordshire egg stand.
Museum of London.

Germany
DORTMUND Museum für Kunst und Kulturgeschichte
DÜSSELDORF Hetjens Museum
DUISBERG Niederrheinisches Museum
FRECHEN Sammlung der Stadt im Rathaus
HAMBURG Museum für kunst und Gewerbe
HÜLS Heimatmuseum
KEVELAER Museum für Niederrheinische Volkskunde
KOMMERN Rheinisches Freilichtmuseum
KREFELD Landeschaftsmuseum des Niederrheins, Burg
Linn
OCHTRUP Sammlung der Stadt

France
BEAUVAIS Musée Departmentale de l'Oise
PARIS Musée des Arts Decoratifs, du Louvre
PARIS Musée des Arts et Traditions Populaire
PARIS Musée de Cluny
SÈVRES Musée National de Céramique

Austria
VIENNA Osterreichisches Museum für Volkskunde

Hungary
BUDAPEST Budapest National Ethnographic Museum

Poland
WARSAW National Ethnographic Museum

Index

References to illustrations are indicated by numerals in *italic* type, and in **bold** type when in colour.